WORK
THE MEANING OF YOUR LIFE

A CHRISTIAN PERSPECTIVE

WORK

THE MEANING OF YOUR LIFE

A CHRISTIAN PERSPECTIVE

LESTER DEKOSTER

Foreword by Stephen J. Grabill

Afterword by Greg Forster

Christian's LIBRARY PRESS

GRAND RAPIDS · MICHIGAN

CHRISTIAN'S LIBRARY PRESS
  *An imprint of the Acton Institute
  for the Study of Religion & Liberty*
98 E. Fulton
Grand Rapids, Michigan 49503
Phone: 616.454.3080
www.clpress.com

Cover design by Esther Moody
Interior composition by Judy Schafer

To Buzz

Lay a blanket of seeds upon a field …
And behold … a harvest!
Lay a blanket of work upon the world …
And behold … a civilization!

CONTENTS

FOREWORD

The staying power of Lester DeKoster's little booklet is due to his foresight in seeing work as a manifestation of whole-life discipleship. You can find countless authors writing about the ills of the workplace, better ways to manage time and resources, daily planning and organizational practices, the moral character of the worker, workplace ethics, and so on, but few ever take up the theological significance of work itself. And even fewer still slow down long enough to reflect on the spirituality *and* economics of work from a macro-level perspective. Not so with Lester DeKoster; he probes these topics with his characteristic wit, keen intellect, and rhetorical acumen. The result is a book with mass appeal and convicting power that is still insightful decades after its original publication.

Why is this the case? It is because he stays focused on a perennial question, "Does work give meaning to life?" His resounding affirmation uncovers three essential insights that make this book a must read for anyone who has ever wondered whether work is really a divine institution and not merely a necessary evil.

The first insight is that work, indeed, gives meaning to life because it is the form in which we make ourselves useful to others, and thus to God. God accomplishes his purposes in the world by equipping us with talents, skills, and abilities that he expects us to use in service to others.

The second insight, building on the collective wisdom of the free-market tradition, is that our work shares in weaving civilization, which is the form in which others make themselves useful to us, by providing us with the tools for doing our work well. This is reminiscent of Adam Smith's famous remark about the brewer, the butcher, and the baker in the *Wealth of Nations* (Bk. III, chap. 1).

And, finally, work sculpts the kind of self we are becoming through the choices we make in the handling of our talents on the job. DeKoster writes: "The chisel we use to sculpt our selves is choice. It's not a chisel of our own making: it's a tool we can't avoid using…. Selves are formed into sheep or goat by the 'god' we serve in the choices we make in all of life."

Evangelicals have always had an implicit sense that work is good because it carries out the cultural mandate, but rarely, if ever, have they thought of work as one of the core elements of discipleship and spiritual formation. In fact, one of the most pressing needs among evangelicals today is to revive a commitment to whole-life discipleship. Christianity is about so much more than what happens for an hour or two on Sunday morning; it's a way of life and it affects every area of our lives, including our working life.

With the passing of Lester DeKoster in 2009, the Acton Institute assumed the leadership of Christian's Library Press, the imprint that Lester DeKoster and Gerard Berghoef founded in 1979. Given the Acton Institute's interest in the relationship between work, stewardship, and economics—in other words, biblical *oikonomia*—it makes sense for us to reissue *Work: The*

Meaning of Your Life in various formats fit for a new generation. This reissue features a new Foreword and Afterword, the latter of which is a reprint of an essay by Greg Forster that first appeared in *The Pastor's Guide to Fruitful Work & Economic Wisdom*, a publication of the Made to Flourish pastors' network. This reissue of *Work* also includes a light edit and update of the text, as well as the alteration of biblical citations from the Revised Standard Version in the original printing to the New International Version of Scripture now in this printing.

My hope is simple: Read and understand, and pray that God will open the windows of heaven to bring about a revolution in seminary education and church life in our day, one that will finally mobilize the whole people of God to grasp the full implication of Colossians 3:23–24: "Whatever you do, work at it with all your heart, as working for the Lord, not for men, since you know that you will receive an inheritance from the Lord as a reward. It is the Lord Christ you are serving."

—Stephen J. Grabill, Ph.D.
Senior Research Scholar in Theology
and Director of Programs
Acton Institute

General Editor
NIV Stewardship Study Bible

PREFACE

Work gets the largest single block of our lives.

Yet we tend to look for meaningful living anywhere but on the job.

We work daily for the paycheck that tries to keep necessity at bay and provides us enough leisure besides to pursue what seems to give meaning to our existence.

We don't quite work just to eat nor eat just to work—at least we don't want to. However, it often comes down near to that, and time on the job is for too many of us time at the rat race—with the rats winning.

Sometimes we pause to wonder: Is this, then, what life amounts to—a wilderness of work broken with oases of meaning furnished by our families, the church, politics, community affairs, plus hobbies and spectator sports thrown in to give some zest to leisure?

Is this "it"?

I used to think so. Do you now?

Not that most of us expect to make some big splash in the news—those who do are soon eclipsed by new faces on our TV screens anyhow. Who was who, just yesterday? We do crave sensing, somehow, that we count for more than we can control with our income or do with our spare time. Our hearts whisper that life *must* have some meaning besides the poet's "getting and spending...."

One day two things dawned on me: (1) If life is to have meaning, I would have to find it, not hope to create it for myself. (2) Living must get its meaning, first of all, on the job, because that's the drain down which the best hours of every week dribble away.

At first, these options seemed fanciful: Life's meaning on the job? Not because I put it there, but because *work* endows living with significance? Kidding somebody?

No kidding at all. That's the way it is. Come along and see for yourself!

Looking back, I noticed that I had made this little adventure in perception without going anywhere in particular—leading me also to think that the most important journeys we can take are those that shift our outlook, right at home. Not too far to travel!

I write this booklet so that you can share, if you want to, the same discovery: It *is* your daily work, whatever your job, that does give meaning to your life, not because you will now decide to put meaning there but because God has already done so.

And what, by the way, is meant here by "meaning"?

Meaning is the answer to the "what fors" of life. Why work? Why play? Why do anything at all? What is it all about? Such queries probe for meaning, no less in the lives of the jet set than in those of the frustrated and poor. Meaning gets rounded out, of course, beyond the job—in our families, our religious and community activities, our friends, and on vacations, dabbling with our hobbies, and so forth. However, working takes the core of the week for most of us, and if the job drains life of meaning then all else is shadowed too—how heavy hangs next Monday morning over the whole weekend for the many who loathe their jobs.

If work can give a central core of meaning to living, then all other meanings cluster around this one.

Therefore, a right view of work becomes the key to a satisfying life, as it now looks to me. And whenever, and wherever, I see people working—at any kind of work, such as head or hand, blue-collar or white-collar, trade or profession—I want to shout out the good news: *This* gives meaning to your life! Right here! Right now!

Come and see.

1

WHAT IS WORK?

Work Is the Form in Which We Make Ourselves Useful to Others

The Secret

This is really the open secret of all that follows: *Work is the form in which we make ourselves useful to others.*

I'm not saying that's the way I always looked at my jobs. I'm not saying that's how you should look at yours now. But that is, I am convinced, the essence of working: making ourselves useful to others.

That is why work gives meaning to life.

Work means here, remember, everybody's job, from that paid in executive salaries and bonuses to that unpaid in the kitchen; from that measured by the peck or the bushel or the yard to that calculated by hourly rates or piece counts; work ranging from lawyering to flying jet liners, from office to assembly line, from White House to sweat shop. In short, by *work* I mean whatever people do to earn their living. No matter what the job is, its essence is unchanging: Work is the form in which we make ourselves useful to others.

Work creates civilization and culture (we will use both terms to indicate the same thing). The difference between life in the African bush and life in the Western world is *work*.

Don't African bush people work?

Yes, but at a primitive level. The bush people have to do everything for themselves. Civilization is sharing in the work of others.

It is a circle we will finally see close: Our working puts us in the service of others; the civilization that work creates puts others in the service of ourselves. Thus, work restores the broken family of humankind.

Why?

Because through work that serves others, we also serve God, and he in exchange weaves the work of others into a culture that makes our work easier and more rewarding.

As seed multiplies into a harvest under the wings of the Holy Spirit, so work multiplies into a civilization under the intricate hand of that same Spirit.

This is why work gives meaning to your life and to mine.

The Power

We know, as soon as reminded, that work spins the wheels of the world.

No work? Then nothing else either. Culture and civilization don't just happen. They are made to happen and to keep happening—by God the Holy Spirit, *through our work*.

Imagine that everyone quits working, right now! What happens? Civilized life quickly melts away. Food vanishes from the store shelves, gas pumps dry up, streets are no longer patrolled, and fires burn themselves out. Communication and transportation services end and utilities go dead. Those who survive at all are soon huddled around campfires, sleeping in tents, and clothed in rags.

The difference between barbarism and culture is, simply, work. One of the mystifying facts of history is why certain people create progressive cultures while others lag behind. Whatever that explanation, the power lies in work.

Another interesting thing is that if all workers did quit, it would not make too much difference which workers quit first—front office, boardroom, assembly line, or custodial staff. Civilized living is so closely knit that when any pieces drop out the whole fabric begins to crumple. Let city sanitation workers go out this week, and by next week streets are smothered in garbage. Give homemaking mothers leave, and many of us suddenly go hungry and see our kids running wild. Civilization is so fragile that we either all hang together or, as Ben Franklin warned during the American Revolution, "we shall all hang separately."

Incidentally, let's not make the mistake, if ever we are tempted, of estimating the importance of our work, or of any kind of work, by the public esteem it enjoys. Up-front types make news, but only workers create civilized life. The mosaic of culture, like all mosaics, derives its beauty from the contribution of each tiny bit.

The Harvest

As seeds multiply themselves into harvest, so work flowers into civilization. The second harvest parallels the first: Civilization, like the fertile fields, yields far more in return on our efforts than our particular jobs put in.

Verify that a moment by taking a casual look around the room in which you are now sitting. Just how long would it have taken you to make, piece by piece, the things you can lay eyes on?

Let's look together.

That chair you are lounging in? Could you have made it for yourself? Well, I suppose so, *if* we mean just the chair!

Perhaps you did in fact go out to buy the wood, the nails, the glue, the stuffing, the springs—and put it all together. But if by making the chair we mean assembling each part *from scratch*, that's quite another matter. How do we get, say, the wood? Go and fell a tree? But only after first making the tools for that, and putting together some kind of vehicle to haul the wood, and constructing a mill to do the lumber, and roads to drive on from place to place? In short, a lifetime or two to make one chair! We are physically unable, it is obvious, to provide ourselves from scratch with the household goods we can now see from wherever you and I are sitting—to say nothing of building and furnishing the whole house.

Consider everything else that we can use every day and never really see. Who builds and maintains the roads and streets we take for granted? Who polices them so we can move about in comparative safety? Who erects the stores, landscapes the parks, builds the freeways? Who provides the services that keep things going in good weather and bad?

Well, civilization blends work into doing all that. It's what we mean by civilization, really—goods and services to hand when we need them. There are countless workers, just like ourselves—including ourselves—whose work creates the harvest that provides each of us with far more than we could ever provide for ourselves.

Going shopping? Someone's work has already stocked the aisles with food, stuffed the racks with clothing, crowded counters with goods—for you!

Going traveling? Someone's work has already paved the highways, built the airports, designed and fueled the planes—for you!

Going abroad? Someone's work has already raised the cathedrals, painted the pictures, laid out the cities—for you!

Staying home? Someone's work enlivens TV channels, prints the daily paper, keeps social order—for you!

In trouble? Someone's work defies emergencies, defeats the storms, and has repairs ready—for you!

So everywhere and at all times, there are countless hands moving all the wheels of civilization—for you!

Work plants the seed; civilization reaps the harvest. Work is the form in which we make ourselves useful to others; civilization is the form in which others make themselves useful to us. We plant; God gives the increase to unify the human race.

Forgotten Something?

Oh, I know, you think I've forgotten something, and before you take a look around you want to be sure it's counted in.

You're thinking that what I've been saying is sentimental, as if some celestial Santa Claus dropped everything into my living room by way of the chimney. In fact, nothing is free in this old world? Pay for whatever you want, or do without it? No two ways about that!

So, then, I'm forgetting that I've *paid* for whatever it is that I own and pay my share in taxes and profits for all the public and private services I enjoy? This is what you think I've ignored? No paycheck, nothing else?

Well, no, I thought of that—and read quite a few books on economics, from old Adam Smith to Karl Marx to Kenneth Galbraith to discover just how my paycheck does relate to all those things I own and use.

Funny thing, though, these experts didn't help much.

It's too simple for the experts, probably.

As I see it now, things stand like this: Our paychecks represent our working efforts in, say, forty hours per week. Some bring in far more dollars than others, but just say that on the average each should in fact buy only what you or I could make for ourselves in the same forty hours a week. (Economics is not that simple? Maybe not, but for now let it pass—because when you start looking seriously at the meaning of civilization, my way is how you will see it, too, I think).

At least we can agree that if we both worked not only forty but, say, one hundred and forty hours a week, we ourselves couldn't make from scratch even a fraction of all the goods and services that we call our own. A funny thing happens, as they used to say, to a paycheck on its way to the bank. That paycheck turns out to buy us the use of far more than we could possibly make for ourselves in the time it takes us to earn the check. Money is the key that opens the storehouse of civilization, but a whole lot more comes flooding out through that door than we could make for ourselves in the time it takes to earn the key.

And that's true, no matter how big the check becomes.

The experts, I say, don't seem to explain that exactly.

But that's the way it is.

Goods and Services

We can profit from one useful distinction made by the experts: They talk about *goods* and *services* as the forms taken by work.

So our jobs can be divided between those that produce goods and those that render services.

Goods are things that last while services pass with the doing. The stove in your kitchen belongs to the world's goods; the cooking done on it adds to the world's services. The desk in my office is among economic goods; the work done over it joins economic services.

The reason for taking note of this distinction is to parry in advance the mistake of thinking that work invested in goods is more important than work invested in services. Goods do seem to congeal and preserve the labor invested in them, while services pass with the moment of performance.

True but misleading, because goods without attendant services do not amount to much, nor do they last very long.

A great cathedral endures, it is true, for centuries, immortalizing the hands that made it; while work spent in sweeping its floors seems to disappear with the swish of the broom. However, a building left unattended and uncared for soon serves no one but those interested in ruins. Your car unserviced, a highway unrepaired, the television set untouched, the stove left cold—such goods soon play no constructive role in civilization.

Goods and services are twins. Work invested in either knits the robe of culture. Without goods services are inept; without services goods are lame.

For Others

Our definition of work as the form in which we make ourselves useful to others is, by the way, sober economics, not some poetaster's fancy.

Goods and services are not produced as ends in themselves. Either they benefit others or there is no demand for their doing. That is to say, either they sell because they are useful to others or no one hires us to produce them.

We find work to do, in fact, only because what we do is useful, that is salable, to another.

Therefore, we can repeat that work gives meaning to life *because* work is the way in which we make ourselves useful to society.

If you still find that hard to "see," so once did I.

I found it even harder to "see" that work could even be called the "gift" of my self to the benefit of another. Before we are through, though, we just might want to insist on that—wait and see. (We will not forget to ask how this relates to the paycheck.)

Summary

All of our efforts to endow our lives with meaning are apt to come up short and disappointing. Why? Because all our passion to fill the meaning-vacuum through multiplied activity in the home, the church, the community, or whatever stumbles over that big block of every week's time we have to spend on the seeming meaninglessness of the job. The spare-time charities cannot tip the scales. Redoubling our efforts only obscures the goal.

We are sometimes advised to try giving meaning to our work (instead of finding it there) by thinking of the job in religious terms such as *calling* or *vocation*. What seems at first like a helpful perspective, however, deals with work as if from the outside. We find ourselves still trying to endow our own work with meaning. We are trying to find the content in the label, without real success. The meaning we seek has to be *in* work itself.

And so it is!

2

WORD ON WORK

The Day of Illumination

Why?

Work gives meaning to life because work is the form in which we make ourselves useful to others.

Why should this be a source of meaning?

Why does serving others give meaning to life?

We can reply that the work that places us in the service of others shares in the creation of civilization, the form in which others put themselves in our service. We get because we give—which lends meaning to giving.

This might be more than ground enough for finding meaning in working, but we can still ask: Why does God the Holy Spirit weave our work into civilization, much as he multiplies the planting of seeds into a harvest?

The answer is twofold: First, God himself chooses to be served through the work that serves others and therefore molds working into culture to provide workers with even better means of service. Second, God has so made us that through working we actually sculpt the kind of selves we each are becoming, in time and for eternity.

Both of these perspectives on the meaning of work are illumined by two familiar parables told by Jesus.

The first is commonly called the parable of the Last Judgment and the second the parable of the talents.

Judgment by Illumination

The following account of the Last Judgment reflects God's attitude toward work. The Lord says:

> "When the Son of Man comes in his glory, and all the angels with him, he will sit on his throne in heavenly glory. All the nations will be gathered before him, and he will separate the people one from another as a shepherd separates the sheep from the goats. He will put the sheep on his right and the goats on his left.
>
> "Then the King will say to those on his right, 'Come, you who are blessed by my Father; take your inheritance, the kingdom prepared for you since the creation of the world. For I was hungry and you gave me something to eat, I was thirsty and you gave me something to drink, I was a stranger and you invited me in, I needed clothes and you clothed me, I was sick and you looked after me, I was in prison and you came to visit me.'
>
> "Then the righteous will answer him, 'Lord, when did we see you hungry and feed you, or thirsty and give you something to drink? When did we see you a stranger and invite you in, or needing clothes and clothe you? When did we see you sick or in prison and go to visit you?'
>
> "The King will reply, 'I tell you the truth, whatever you did for one of the least of these brothers of mine, you did for me.'
>
> "Then he will say to those on his left, 'Depart from me, you who are cursed, into the eternal fire prepared for the devil and his angels. For I was hungry and you gave me nothing to eat, I was thirsty and you gave me nothing to drink, I was a stranger and you did not invite me in, I

needed clothes and you did not clothe me, I was sick and in prison and you did not look after me.'

"They also will answer, 'Lord, when did we see you hungry or thirsty or a stranger or needing clothes or sick or in prison, and did not help you?'

"He will reply, 'I tell you the truth, whatever you did not do for one of the least of these, you did not do for me.'

"Then they will go away to eternal punishment, but the righteous to eternal life."

—Matt. 25:31–46

Work and Judgment

The parable just quoted illumines why God the Holy Spirit weaves our work into the fabric of civilization.

I did not always read the parable that way. Once it seemed to commend special acts of giving, such as charities that we ought to be doing in our spare time.

The Lord does not specify when or where the good deeds he blesses are done, but it now seems to me that Jesus is obviously speaking of more than a vocational behavior or pastime kindnesses. Why? Because he hinges our entire eternal destiny upon giving ourselves to the service of others—and that can hardly be a pastime event. In fact, giving our selves to the service of others, as obviously required by the Lord, is precisely what the central block of life that we give to working turns out to be!

Is the Lord talking here about *work*?

Yes, I've come to think so.

Notice that the Day described in the parable might as readily be called the Day of Illumination as the Day of Judgment.

When were the sheep separated from the goats? Was it after the Lord had pronounced his judgment upon all those assembled before him? Did he, so to speak, weigh credits versus debits, pass judgment, and then proceed to separate the sheep from the goats?

11

The separation of sheep from goat is not made *after* the Lord's judgment is announced. The awful separation has taken place *before* a word is spoken: "All the nations will be gathered before him, and he will separate the people one from another as a shepherd separates the sheep from the goats. He will put the sheep on his right and the goats on his left. Then the King will say …" (Matt. 25:32–34).

First, the division; then, the explanation! Before the Lord says a word, the separation has been made. In fact, it is clear that the Judge does not make that division at all; he simply confirms it. The sheep got to the throne as already sheep; the goats got to the throne as already goats. Those who arrived as "sheep" are guided by angels to the Judge's right hand; those who arrived as "goats" are herded to his left! *Before*, mind you, a word is said! Sheep and goats are gathered with their kind *first of all*, and then what happens?

Only then, come the words of judgment.

No, not so much the words of judgment as the words of explanation! The Judge explains how those before him had qualified themselves for positioning on the right or left of his throne. Becoming sheep or goat has a history, one made by each sheep or goat for himself or herself. Each is told what he or she has spent life in becoming—and how. The parable is teaching us that we will "see" at last what day-by-day living is all about. It's a matter of becoming sheep or becoming goat. *That* is the meaning of time spent on the job and of time spent on all else.

The dividing line in all such becoming is starkly obvious: the willingness (sheep) or the refusal (goat) to give of ourselves to the service of others!

But giving self to the service of others—*that's what work is!*

"I Was ..." and You ...

I was hungry and you gave me something to eat.

The Lord is saying that where humans are hungry, there he too chooses to hunger. He waits in the hungry man or woman or child, longing to be served. Served how? By the work of those who knit the garment of civilization through the production and distribution of food!

God himself, hungering in the hungry, is served by all those who work in ...

- · agriculture,
- · wholesale or retail foods,
- · kitchens or restaurants,
- · food transportation or the mass production of food items,
- · manufacturing of implements used in agriculture or in any of the countless food-related industries,
- · innumerable support services and enterprises that together make food production and distribution possible.

God transforms plantings into harvests. Then he waits to be fed by those whose work turns harvests into one of the basic elements of civilization. The gift of ourselves to others through work *is* the gift of ourselves to God—and this is why work gives both temporal and eternal meaning to life!

I was thirsty and you gave me something to drink.

This parable was not composed at random. Jesus is getting at the basic necessities that civilization provides to human life—first food, now water. And God is served by those whose work contributes to the availability, distribution, and use of water—be it to slake the thirst of man, beast, or field; be it to keep the world fresh and clean and sanitary. The Lord is "thirsty" wherever water is needed and is served by all who knit the sleeve of civilization by working in ...

· municipal or private water services,
· purifying waters,
· exploration for or desalinization of water,
· well-drilling, pipe-laying, plumbing installation, or maintenance,
· manufacturing or servicing water-related equipment,
· working in the countless water-related goods and service industries.

The God who through the cycle of evaporation and return replenishes the earth's water supply waits on the service of those whose work refreshes the thirsty with life-giving water. The gift of ourselves to civilized life through our work *is* the gift of ourselves to God.

I needed clothes and you clothed me.

The third and last of the basic necessities that work contributes to civilization is clothing and shelter.

Jesus is indeed talking about far more than part-time and perhaps incidental charities in this parable. He is obviously talking about the civilization created by the world's work. The scope of the parable embraces all the work required to provide the physical necessities of culture.

Here Jesus is saying: I was in all who need shelter and clothing, and you are working in ...

· textiles,
· building and repairing of dwellings,
· sales of clothing and shelter items,
· fire or police or military protection of property,
· real estate and insurance,
· the (who knows how many) goods and service occupations related to shelter and comfort.

The Lord's choice of the kinds of services that are instanced in the parable is carefully calculated to comprehend a vast number of the jobs of humankind. The parable is about the work needed to provide the sinews of civilization. Doing such work, the Lord says, is serving his purposes in history, and in exchange he rewards workers far beyond their input with all the abundance of culture's storehouse.

"I Am ..." and You ...

You will notice a change in the caption from "I Was ..." to "I Am ..."

To stress a point!

The parable speaks in terms of time past. From the parable's point of view, it's all over. Time has been rolled up like a scroll. All the world's clocks have stopped, the bells are silent, and alarms sound no more. The trial period is ended. Life has been lived. Judge and the judged are looking back upon the irremediable. Sheep *are* sheep; goats *are* goats. Nothing left but finding that out.

Happily, for us it is not yet so!

It was not only yesterday that the Lord waited in the persons whom we can aim to serve through our work, but it is right now, today. "Now" is, in fact, all the time we ever have. We may remember the past and anticipate the future, but we live only and always in the "now," the "today." And so, the apostle cautions us, "Today, if you hear his voice, do not harden your hearts ..." (Heb. 3:15; quoting Ps. 95:7–8). Now is the moment to perceive that work relates us to God because it involves us in civilization. God uses our work to create and sustain culture. That, we may say again, is why work gives meaning to life!

The parable does not stop with the basic physical necessities of existence. "Man does not live on bread alone" (Deut. 8:3; quoted by Jesus in Matt. 4:4). The Lord now goes on to include other facets of culture, also created through work—so

15

that, finally, the parable embraces all that work of any kind provides.

I was sick and you looked after me.

Human health, for example, thrives on the boundary between the physical and the mental. And the Lord says, "I was sick," and you work in ...

- · medical services,
- · counseling, visiting, healing,
- · the making or selling of medicines or in related research,
- · health insurance,
- · serving others through working in any of the numerous physical or mental health-related occupations.

Psychosomatic health merges into spiritual health, a wholeness nurtured in communion with each other. To be human is to be in relation with others. Such communion is facilitated by love and communication. Indeed, communication and spiritual concern unify civilization. Culture means togetherness, a togetherness served by countless human occupations.

I was a stranger and you invited me in.

"I was a stranger," the Lord says, for all who seek communion and communication, and you work ...

- · for a telephone company,
- · at delivering the mail,
- · in the church,
- · at keeping cars moving, roads open, and commercial means of travel running,
- · in the media and TV,
- · in any of the innumerable avenues of service that keep people in communication with each other and the world.

I was in prison and you came to visit me.

God chooses to be found also among social "outcasts," those whom Franz Fannon called "The Wretched of the Earth"—those literally imprisoned, the hurt (also on their jobs), and those mentally or physically held hostage by ignorance, fear, exploitation, tyranny; and you work in …

- · social services, professional or voluntary,
- · law or the courts on behalf of justice,
- · education,
- · politics and government,
- · providing employment,
- · human rehabilitation,
- · any of the liberating services that so many desperately need.

Including Your Own

Have we missed the particular kind of work you do?

Not surprising. There are thousands of occupations.

Recall, though, that the parable is designed to include the world's work, and the world's workers—all who do "socially useful" labor.

In this revealed light, it is clear why work not only gives meaning to life in time but to life for eternity. "To work," St. Benedict said, "is to pray!"

And we may add, "To work is to love—both God and neighbor!"

For the "love" required by the Bible is the service of God through the service of man.

And because God wills to be served through our service of others, he provides us with civilization to facilitate our working at our best.

Intention

Now a problem: If to work is to love, what then is the basis of the Lord's separation between "sheep" and "goats"?

Did only the sheep work? That is hardly likely.

1. There are those making themselves goats by working at jobs on which the Lord does *not* depend, work which sullies culture with the grime of lawlessness, selfishness, and greed—jobs that destroy rather than weave the fabric of civilization. Such work sculpts a self destined for eternal rejection.

2. We are going to observe in a moment that there is a ratio between the talents that God invests in us and how well we use them at work. This ratio plays a role in sculpting us into sheep or goat.

3. No doubt, sheep also separate from goats in the very purpose and intent for which they really work. Why do the job? For others, or for self alone? What is our aim in life? The Lord may be served by those who in fact work with self-interest only in view, who do the very least they can get away with and as poorly as the traffic will bear, taking as much and returning as little as possible—but he is served, then, as it were by accident and against the worker's intention. Surely, these become goats perhaps without knowing how or why. Sheep differs from goat, say in "set of sail" or "point of compass" or, simply, "what am I really *after*?"

4. Then there are those whose work really accomplishes so little that their paycheck is a form of welfare. They claim the fruits of civilization while investing little of themselves in return—thus staking out a claim to space on the left of the throne.

5. And, of course, there are goats who count it clever not to work—perhaps skimming off the goods of culture through clipping coupons, or making do on skid row. Goats in dinner jackets or goats in rags. "I was hungry ..." and what did *you* do about it?

Perhaps the goats are surprised on that Day of Illumination because it never occurred to them that work had anything to do with the service of God! How were they to know that working—or not working—solely with their own self-interest in view was robbing God himself!

The sheep express surprise also. Was their job, nameless and insignificant as it appeared to them, *really* serving God?! And now rewarded far beyond human dreams?

Yes, just so!

Review briefly the parable again:

1. Those on the Lord's right hand put themselves there by serving the needs of others. This is what working does. What surprises them is that in so doing they were serving God himself.

2. Those on the Lord's left hand put themselves there by refusing to work at serving the needs of others, or neglecting to exploit the talents with which God endowed them. Perhaps they worked at jobs that did violence to the will of God and good of man; perhaps they never worked at all; perhaps they worked with an eye solely to self-interest, got by with whatever they could, and grabbed every key to the storehouse door that they could lay hands on by fair means or by foul. What frustrates them is the belated perception that it was God whom they were robbing in their abuse of man. It was the store of goods and services that God intended for all humankind that the goats pillaged for themselves.

The sobering import of this parable is that, in the end, both sheep and goats are simply guided to the place they have been seeking all their lives: sheep are led to the company of the Lord they served, perhaps unknowingly; goats are assigned the place where goats could alone belong—among their kind, in the alienation from each other and from God that they practiced in life. This is, by the way, the theme of Italian poet Dante's great dramatic work, *The Divine Comedy*.

We go, the great poet teaches, for eternity, exactly where we have been "aiming" to go all our lives—to the blessed union with others and with God to which we have been giving our selves, or to the alienation from God and others which we have so calculatingly practiced.

The account of that great Day of Illumination sets our work in the light of divine revelation—now!

3

WORD ON SELF

Each His Own Artist

Sculpting Selves

It becomes evident through the parable we have just been considering that work shares in the creation of more than goods and services.

Work plays a large role in the sculpting of our selves.

Recall that both sheep and goats arrived at the glorious throne without luggage—no trappings of learning, of academic degrees, of wealth, or of power. None of the scars of poverty either. Everything, much or little, has been left behind. Death strips us of all but our selves. Each comes only as sculpted into sheep or goat. How "sculpted"? Through choosing, moment by moment, for the service of others or for the sole service of self. So the parable obviously teaches. Nothing else matters any longer. All the world's distinctions are blurred out, the fame has faded, the applause no longer rings, diamonds no longer glitter, servants no longer bow and scrape, poverty no longer gnaws, failure no longer nags. The fearful no longer cringe; the proud no longer dominate. Only selves, guided to one hand or the other of the celestial Judge.

"Naked I came from my mother's womb," Job cries, "and naked I will depart"—which furnished the title for the play, *You Can't Take It with You.* No, we can't! Nothing comes along but our selves—the exception which is everything!

We are apt to forget that one by-product of our working is the self we are fashioning, day by day, on the job. Indeed, that self is in fact by far the most important product we produce in the life and time granted us by divine grace.

The chisel we use to sculpt our selves is choice. It's not a chisel of our own making; it's a tool we can't avoid using. To live is to choose—even when we decline to choose, that is itself a choice. Selves are formed into sheep or goat by the "god" we serve in the choices we make in all of life. Do we choose what to think, what to say, what to do in obedience to our Creator's will? Or, do we choose in obedience to self, or to any of the many other beguiling disguises worn by the Devil? We are always in the service of some "master"—ultimately, in the service of God or of his Adversary. Obedience to God's will sculpts sheep, while rebellion molds goats. And because work looms so large in a lifetime, the choices we make on the job play a decisive role in what kind of selves we are becoming.

How do we sculpt our selves on the job? We do it with the chisel of choice, day by day. How well do we choose to do the work at hand? How well do we choose to develop and to use the talents God has given us? What is the quantity and the quality of the work we choose to turn out, every hour? How do we choose—as employer or as employee—to relate to others on the job?

Choice at work in sculpting the self is illumined by a second of our Lord's parables, which we will view from the perspective of "ratio." What is the *ratio* God expects us, by choice, to maintain between the talents that he has invested in us and the use we make of them in working? (How we use our talents elsewhere than on the job falls outside our focus here.)

Ratio

Here is a guide to sculptors—of selves! The Lord says:

"Again, it will be like a man going on a journey, who called his servants and entrusted his property to them. To one he gave five talents of money, to another two talents, and to another one talent, each according to his ability. Then he went on his journey. The man who had received the five talents went at once and put his money to work and gained five more. So also, the one with the two talents gained two more. But the man who had received the one talent went off, dug a hole in the ground and hid his master's money.

"After a long time the master of those servants returned and settled accounts with them. The man who had received the five talents brought the other five. 'Master,' he said, 'you entrusted me with five talents. See, I have gained five more.'

"His master replied, 'Well done, good and faithful servant! You have been faithful with a few things; I will put you in charge of many things. Come and share your master's happiness!'

"The man with the two talents also came. 'Master,' he said, 'you entrusted me with two talents; see, I have gained two more.'

"His master replied, 'Well done, good and faithful servant! You have been faithful with a few things; I will put you in charge of many things. Come and share your master's happiness!'

"Then the man who had received the one talent came. 'Master,' he said, 'I knew that you are a hard man, harvesting where you have not sown and gathering where you have not scattered seed. So I was afraid and went out and hid your talent in the ground. See, here is what belongs to you.'

"His master replied, 'You wicked, lazy servant! So you knew that I harvest where I have not sown and gather where I have not scattered seed? Well then, you should have put my money on deposit with the bankers, so that when I returned I would have received it back with interest.

"'Take the talent from him and give it to the one who has the ten talents. For everyone who has will be given more, and he will have an abundance. Whoever does not have, even what he has will be taken from him. And throw that worthless servant outside, into the darkness, where there will be weeping and gnashing of teeth.'"

—Matt. 25:14–30

Ratio Explained

The parable illumines the ratio that God requires between the talents he has on loan to us, and our sculpting of our selves through the use of his gifts in work that serves him.

Consider the following:

1. The Master distributes what the servants have to work with. All is on loan. So with us, God provides (a) our talents and aptitudes, and (b) the tools of civilization to facilitate our working with his gifts.

2. All initiative rests with the servants. How they employ their talents is up to them. No one to blame but themselves.

3. The Master's intent is obvious: service. That is why each of the recipients of his largesse is called *servant*.

4. The servants have the initiative but can anticipate a final accounting of their stewardship. We, too, are responsible but not independent agents. God waits in final judgment—or final illumination—on the kind of self each of us sculpts through our use of his talents.

5. The faithful servant is expected to work, you noticed, at full capacity. That, then, is the ratio that God blesses—*full* use of whatever talents we are given. Five-talent people are required to turn in a five-talent performance; so also with two-talent folk, and so on. His is the choice as to our talents; ours is the duty to use them to the fullest.

6. Notice, too, that the eye of heaven sees work in its essence, and takes small account of differences among jobs that we think are very important. Five-talent people look very "successful" by all worldly standards, stirring their pride and our envy; one-talent people risk our contempt and their own despair. But in the Master's eye "ratio" levels us all. He pronounces the very same commendation on the work of the two-talented servant as he does on that of the five-talented: "Well done, good and faithful servant; you have been faithful *over a little....*" No ground for pride; no excuse for envy. What counts in the Master's sight is the ratio between gift and performance. Why? Because in that ratio lies the index to the kind of self each is sculpting.

How well am I doing what my job requires? How persistently am I reaching out to do it better? That's his concern. At issue is ratio, between gift and performance.

7. Note that each of the faithful servants received the same reward: "enter into the joy of your master." The self sculpted through work well done in the public eye, like that of famous and successful people, will receive its due reward at the Last Day. The self sculpted through work done in the most unknown of places by the most unrecognized of workers, will receive its due reward at the Last Day. The same glorious prospect opens for both: the "joy" of the Master: "No eye has seen, no ear has heard, no mind has conceived what God has prepared for those who love him," the Apostle writes (1 Cor. 2:9).

8. It's always a matter of ratio: How well do we serve God's purposes in the world with the talents he has on loan to us?

9. And there is that third chap, the ground-digging type. Loafer? Playboy? Shrewdy? Unwilling to venture the use of his skills lest he benefit neighbor, or Master, both in his view undeserving. No intention of using his talent for the advantage of the Giver through the service of those where the Giver wills to be found. His excuse has a familiar ring: Why should I be

using my energies for anybody else? What do I owe anyone? Why let another reap what he has not planted and harvest any benefits from my efforts? Here is the goat in the making, crouched over talents deeply buried in the ground.

The end result of the "ratio" we daily establish between our talents and our work shows up all along the way in the self we are fashioning, the developing sheep or goat. In the end, the talents are recalled; the goods or services our working with them has made are left behind. Only the self we have sculpted travels on alone and exposed to that inevitable appointment with the Master and his angels.

Oh yes, work gives meaning to life: It is the form in which we make ourselves useful to others, and thus to God. It shares in weaving civilization, which is the form in which others make themselves useful to us by providing us with the tools for doing our work well, and it sculpts the kind of self we are becoming through the choices we make in the handling of our talents on the job.

Talents Are for Use

The Bible takes a hard line on the loafer.

Loafers come in several varieties. Some, by inheritance, need not work—and don't! Some, by indisposition, avoid in every way doing the work they are paid for getting done. Some, by preference, panhandle. On all such loafers, and any others, God takes a grim stand.

Just as the master did on the servant who hid his talent in the ground.

God invests in us for return! For 100 percent return, as we have already observed.

"If a man will not work," St. Paul instructs, "he shall not eat" (2 Thess. 3:10).

So much for those who foolishly presume that the world owes us a living or that the love required of Christians includes supporting the scrounger. Work, if you can, or starve! God is no sentimentalist!

God does indeed display, throughout the Bible, great concern for the poor. He hears their cries, and severely condemns those who exploit them. But the poor God loves are, as is evident from St. Paul's rule requiring work in order to eat, the unwilling poor, those who are in need because they cannot find, or cannot do, work.

The Bible views refusal to work as theft: "He who has been stealing must steal no longer, but must work, doing something useful with his own hands, that he may have something to share with those in need" (Eph. 4:28).

Work is a duty.

Why?

Because God loans talents for the purpose of reaping return.

Or, to put it another way: God loans us talents to enable us to choose the kind of self we will sculpt through using them.

A Footnote

There is work, of course, which no society needs. The goods and services produced violate the civil or the moral codes that make civilization possible.

Such work confers no benefit upon the world and therefore gives no meaning to the life of the worker.

We need say no more about it.

Notice, too, that work can be distinguished from play.

We may expend a lot of energy in playing, but we do that for ourselves. Play is fun and relaxing, because it is always an end in itself. The desire that leads to playing is satisfied in the doing.

When playing is done for the benefit of another, such as participation in professional sports, then such play has become work.

Because work is whatever we do for another.

In a word, whatever we do for ourselves, even if we give all kinds of time and energy to it, is play.

What we do in the production of goods and services, of use to others, is work.

4

WALKING WOUNDED

To Survive the Day

Wounds

We have been looking at work—so to speak—work at large and work in general.

What about work in particular? Your job and mine?

Radio columnist Studs Terkel has authored a large volume of interviews with workers in many kinds of jobs (entitled simply *Working*, Pantheon Books, 1974), and concludes that "To survive the day is triumph enough for the walking wounded among us." Terkel is thinking of both nonprofessional and professional, of blue-collar and white-collar, of assembly line and service workers—whose interviews he molds into fascinating and instructive reading. Work, he finds, is for many people a daily wounding experience, time spent under fire.

I have had some tutors of my own on the dark side of the job. They have been adults who have turned up over a number of years to take evening speech classes that I taught for local labor unions. What a collection I might also compile of stories of blasted hopes and maimed spirits as recounted in sometimes halting tones from the speech platform. Hurt suffered to keep the job surfaced in face and gesture as the tales were told.

Terkel is not mistaken. Work can wound.

You may know many workers, and may be one of them, who find nothing wrong with their work. We've all known, or heard of, retirees who can't keep from drifting back, time and again, to where they spent their working lives, forlorn without the routine. If you are one of those who is happy on the job, rejoice in it! But keep your heart open to others not so blessed.

I judge from my listening and from reports like Terkel's, that "wounds" at work are not selective; they can afflict all types of jobs. There is as much grim frustration in the front office as there is on the line. The machine operator may worry about risking a limb while his boss frays his nerves; so the one stops off for a beer on the way home, while the other keeps dates with the shrink. It may be just as boring for executives to jet around the world on expense accounts (glamorous as they appear to most of us) as for others to be trapped by television in the living room. Probably nobody cares much more about anyone else across the swank condominium swimming pool than on the night shift. There are "wounds" enough to go around, and they come in wide variety.

For Example

Here's a brief sampling of some of the kinds of hurts I've seen through the eyes of workers responsible enough to take evening classes after a day on the job (seeking, of course, escape into a "better" one):

Call Me Nemo

Captain Nemo is a character in an adventure tale by Jules Verne, one of the early science fiction writers. Nemo commands a submarine that travels "twenty thousand leagues under the sea" (the title of Verne's book)—written when there were no submarines!

Nemo was carefully chosen. It means "No Name."

Captain No Name! This becomes useful to the story when enemies are trying to identify the mysterious underseas ship by the custom of asking the captain's name.

Drop the "Captain" and that's about the way a lot of workers seem to feel on their jobs—just call me "Nobody"!

My work makes me anonymous. I'm a number, or a hand—and that's all that counts, my hands. Get 'em here on time, and keep 'em moving!

I'm one more tool, a machine with clothes on—as much in the front office as in the shop. And the company pays more mind to how the real tools get on than it does to me.

Galley Slave?

They used to chain galley slaves to their seats in the boats they rowed, and the overseer kept them going at full speed with a whip.

That's about the way I have to work—and don't be fooled if I happen to have an office and secretary of my own. I'm leased to the job, tied to my desk, wired to my truck cab, enslaved to my delivery route, caught in the web of professional routines, a pawn on the world economic chessboard. I'm free on weekends; in the evenings I'm too tired to care about freedom.

Who Cares?

What hurts is that no one seems to care—and I find myself not caring about anybody else either; don't want to be bothered, got troubles enough of my own.

Who cares if I'm happy or tired or lonely or worried? Nobody does!

Are my kids good or bad, well or sick? Who even wants to know if I have kids!

Nobody wants to care. Nobody wants anybody else to want him to care.

Who cares?

Do you *really* want to know?

Who Was I?

I sometimes wonder who I was when I took this job. What did I look forward to before getting trapped by the mortgage and the pension plan and seniority? What was life like before I started moving "up," as I thought, toward the top—only to be greeted by the same old treadmill, carpeted and air conditioned? Who was I then?

And who am I now? As inhuman as the mechanical monster I tend? As dull as the weekly reports I crank out? As programmed as the computers that run me?

I'm burned out, charred before my time. What's going to be left when retirement finally comes? Will I even want to retire? Or enjoy it?

Worst of All

What gets me most of all is the constant put-down. Either being ignored or belittled or griped at. Noticed only when for once I would rather not be noticed, if something goes wrong or I am behind. Come in on time for years, and then catch it for being late once.

Cripples the spirit, this knuckling under all the time. Shrinks you in on yourself, like a puckered lemon. If it were not for the paycheck, or the bonus, or the pension plan—and my debts, I might …

But I'm caught. Bend, take it, or else!

Summary

This is a sampling of hurts on the job, the kind that the "walking wounded" among the world's workers endure. Probably you could expand the list. It covers many people.

Does Christianity take any account of these woundings?

5

WORD ON WOUND

Cross-Bearing

Follow Me

Christianity long ago took full account of the wounds we may suffer at work.

"If anyone would come after me, he must deny himself and take up his cross daily and follow me" (Luke 9:23).

Is the Lord thinking of our time and, for some, hurts on the job?

There is good reason to think so; consider:

To begin with, just giving our time (no one has a limitless stock of it) to working often requires self-denial, sometimes heroic self-denial. That is, most of us have to forego much that we would rather be doing because our working requires so exhausting an investment of both time and energy. It is the grim reality of self-denial that provokes many workers to dreaming of getting out of the factory some day, or away from the office, or free from the kitchen. Only to see those dreams fade as time hastens along, as savings never do accumulate, and as age so quickly turns gray both head and hope!

Yes, the worker—each of us—knows what self-denial is. That's commonly a part of working! Isn't this exactly what the Lord requires of those who would be his followers? Self-denial for self-giving to others—that's what we do through our jobs!

"Take up your cross," the Lord adds.

Wounded workers know by experience what he means! They daily go back to shouldering the cross of unwilling spirits, of complaining muscles, of bone-weary bodies, of aching inner selves, of maimed expectations, of utter frustration—to do the jobs required of them.

What are those wounds suffered on the job, and often carried home besides, but crosses laid upon our shoulders! Indifference? Being taken for granted? No bouquets, ever? Brickbats every now and then? An endless round of drudgery? A cruel and demanding public? Obvious exploitation? No future? Mind-dulling routine? Foul-mouthed associates? Despotic boss? Dishonest employees? Sloppy performance? Customer complaints, all the worse because justified by poor workmanship in the shop? No one catches the vision? No capital?

There is no class or trade monopoly on job-related crosses. "Take up your cross ...," does Jesus command? Countless workers most certainly do!

"And follow me," does he add?

Yes, Lord, we follow—to work!

Again, the Lord says: "For whoever wants to save his life will lose it, but whoever loses his life for me will save it" (Luke 9:24).

And again, obviously applicable to work.

Is it not the "sheep" who willingly surrender life on their own terms to do the job defined in terms of orders issued by others? Is it not the "goat" who twists life, when he can, to conform to his own interest, and in thus "saving" it now loses it forever?

How well workers know what surrendering life's glitter to the gloom of the workplace means!

And as the Lord God surveys his world, what a host of rugged heroes and heroines of labor he must behold! Those who rise with the sun, lifelong, to jobs that demand endless self-sacrifice, and get in return but little reward in pay and still less in recognition. Those who see no sunshine all the day long, in the caverns of the earth or the noisome dungeons of heavy industry. And those—no less heroic—who find their substantial salary and bonuses but small recompense for the burdens, and the envy, their "success" involves. Those who must day by day drive weary bodies and spent minds to one more effort. Those who wrestle with bureaucracy to keep businesses solvent long after patience and pleasure are dead. Some who exercise initiative without appreciation, but persevere well beyond the need for personal monetary reward. Mothers whose lives are poured into their families; fathers whose bodies are sacrificed that their wives and children might live. God sees migrant families struggling hopelessly from dawn to dusk; peasants who grub like slaves without hope; service employees called any time for emergencies, surrendering their family holidays or busy through the dark of night.

"Lose your life ...," is Jesus asking us? He is talking about the martyrdoms of labor too.

Job heroism has no class distinctions, only differing forms. There are frontiers all over our workaday world requiring courage and perseverance as intrepid as ever conquered any geographical frontiers. Frontiers met and bested every day, in the kitchen, in the catacombs of industry, in the glare of the front office, in the high level visibility of the rich and the powerful.

Work can be cross bearing, self-denying, and life-sacrificing; because work is following the Lord in ways of service, be that in ways hidden to all but God alone or at an envied occupation demanding sacrifices only the doer can know.

Yes, the Bible takes full account of the wounds inflicted by working. And God instructs us that in suffering these to give our selves to the service of others, we follow the way set before his followers by the Lord Jesus himself. Christianity is not a detour around life's problems; it leads us along the narrow way of shouldering our cross and becoming "sheep" in the process!

We can, though, see our own work more realistically, too, as a means of facing the burdens it lays upon us.

Let's ask, "What's good about work—yours and mine?"

6

WORKER ON WOUND

Seeing for Ourselves

Perspective

We who work have our own share to do in setting our working in creative perspective. And above all we must constantly remind ourselves that the difference between barbarism and civilization is *work*. Our work joins us in knitting the garment of culture which we ourselves enjoy.

There are other things, such as the following:

1. The fact that work ranges far ahead of politics in bringing the peoples of the globe closer together. The multinational corporations are often the whipping boys of theorists who quietly enjoy the products while they condemn the source. And these massive conglomerates are as far from perfection as most other human inventions. But the multinationals do draw diverse sinews of labor into cooperative and constructive effort which transcends geographic boundaries, penetrates political borders, and even joins East and West, North and South, in the production of goods and services. In this way, international economic enterprise prefigures an international

political cooperation that alone is the true hope for world peace.

When politics does achieve the unifying effect of work, the world may at last enjoy a new era of peace with prosperity. The Marxists are not mistaken in the challenge: "Workers of the world unite!" They are simply mistaken in looking to Communism as the unifying force.

2. Work underlies what we commonly perceive as the highest forms of culture as well as the simplest. Trace back to their sources the noblest creations of human genius: We always come, at last, to some person or persons at work.

Great artists work! Composers work! Inventors work! Just as charismatic political leaders work! And masters of business and industrial enterprise work! Just as do countless ordinary folk like us.

3. The writer who speaks of *Leisure, the Basis of Culture* (Josef Pieper) is confused, even though he can quote some ancient Greek thinkers in his support. Work is the basis of culture. Leisure cultivated as a way of life produces no harvests but only dilettantes—drones that absorb culture without sacrificing for it, merely thieves of others' sweat.

There is one hitch to all this. We come naturally to one question: How dare I believe that my particular job really matters in a world where millions upon millions are working? We may begin a response to that natural query by thinking of the old story about why a great battle was lost. Why? Because a key general was delayed in getting to the front. Why? By his horse going lame. Why? For having cast a shoe. Why? Because nails dropped out. Why? Thanks to the blacksmith—who hammered them into the hoof carelessly. Now, who counted most in causing the defeat? Was it the general, or the smith, or the horse, or the shoe, or the nails? How would you answer that question? Could you, in fact, really answer it? Or does the story say something about the interrelated character of our world—because winning the battle needed them all, in such a way that in fact no one can be quite sure which was most important?

Just as civilization needs the work of all of us in such a way, who can tell which one of us is or is not indispensable?

True enough, in the middle of the job we sometimes want, like a child, to cry out, "Hi, Mom, watch *me*!"

And who's watching?

Let's see!

From Thread to Fabric

The fabric of civilization, like all fabrics, is made up of countless tiny threads—each thread the work of someone. Superficially, any given thread might be readily spared or replaced—that could be my job or yours. Thinking this, we go to work on the margin, so to speak, of culture: Who needs *me*?

Is this so? Is the fact that each of us might never be missed or easily be replaced proof that what we do does not matter?

Not at all!

What matters is that we *do* our work! We are daily providing the threads which join with innumerable others in making civilized life possible.

Consider once again the furniture around you. It's congealed work—and worker. Countless hands fashioned it all along the way from raw material to finished product. Our homes are furnished because there *is* a tightly woven *fabric* of civilization, or there would be no chair, no sofa, no table, and no car, no street, nothing at all. What civilizes our world is the fact that work is done. Somewhere in the whole mosaic of goods and services our work is being done too. My chair would be no more useful were it autographed by every hand that gave something to its creation! I can use it simply because everyone did their job.

Suppose that the rain drops, one after the other, opted out of a shower because, after all, what does one little droplet amount to? By itself, of course, not much. But the drops have to be in there, one by one, to make a shower; and it's the showers that make things grow. No matter that the one tiny drop is anonymous or could in theory be easily replaced. In fact, each drop combines with every other to slake the thirst of the earth.

Wholes are possible only because there are parts!

No drops—no showers. No tiny threads of work, no civilization. Doing the daily job provides the daily thread: *that* is what matters!

If we put a painting under a microscope, it becomes apparent that each color exists thanks to innumerable tiny dots. If we analyze a television screen, it is evident that the figures we see are in fact visible because each is composed of small individual units. And if we could trace our automobiles back through all the steps involved in making them, we would find workers' hands investing workers' selves every step of the way. All wholes are made up of individual parts. What matters, always, is not who can count the parts or how readily each part *could* have been replaced. What matters is that the parts are, each of them, there! What matters is that the job, each job, like yours or mine, has a doer and gets done.

Unless many workers just like ourselves did give themselves to making the chairs we are now sitting on, we would be sitting on the floor. Unless, of course, nobody ever invested himself in making us a floor. Then we would be sitting on the grass out in the backyard—unless nobody ever planted and mowed the grass! In a world without work being *done* by countless and anonymous someones, we would all be Tarzans swinging from tree to tree.

The day we went to work we locked hands with humankind in weaving the texture of civilized life—and our lives each found the key to meaning.

Our thread counts because it is *done*!

Servant of Gadgets

What about the workers (perhaps you are one of them) who are simply slaves to modern invention? Who are controlled by the latest gadgets, by the schedule, or the assembly line, or the computer—like the cuckoo on a clock? The cheery little bird may imagine that it pops out on the hour by its own choice, but we know that the cuckoo is only a slave to the mechanism ticking away below its perch. More and more workers feel that what they might call technological regress inexorably remakes man into the image of the robots it provides. Invention serves humankind, no doubt, but only by forcing more and more workers to serve it!

That's not to be denied, and you may be one of the wounded victims.

What's to be said about that kind of wounding?

Well, what would your own life, and that of the civilized world, be like if technology and its marvelous creations were abandoned? Work would slip from its civilized to its primitive forms, and we all would fall back into barbarism. How quickly life would once again fit the philosopher Hobbes' description of early man's existence, "solitary, poor, nasty, brutish, and short."

That's about our choice: technology or barbarism. Think of the chaos that threatens a city when only one system, electrical power, goes out for a few hours. It's simply far better to be one of the workers tending the needs of a huge mechanical harvester as part of some vast agribusiness than to live in a world where starvation stalks its millions of victims. Technology makes it possible to produce enough food now around the world to feed everyone—the problem has become one of honest distribution. Again, far better, isn't it, for workers to serve all the routines involved in the production of the newest drugs than to live in the era of the witch doctor? Technology has revolutionized civilization, and it promises untold achievements ahead! The work that serves it weaves the fabric of culture.

Technology wounds. No doubt about that. It may be wounding you on the job right now. It may be making you feel absolutely unnecessary, for example, or so necessary as to be running you ragged. Every day is a bruising slavery, and who can do anything about it?

Only you can, both by perceiving your work as giving meaning to your life, and by learning to "see" what constantly advancing technological progress provides, not only for others but no less for you. Thanks to technology and the machine, more persons than ever before in human history enjoy the blessings of culture. The promise of the future is unlimited, especially as work unifies the world. Those who "pay" for technological achievements by serving the robots give just that much more of themselves to cross-bearing for human progress. God is well aware of that, while his Holy Spirit uses your work to create even more miracles in cultural progress.

Many are the unsung warriors on the technological frontiers of human progress, who bear their cross and endure the wounds that the lavish gifts of modern civilization may be extended around the globe.

From Cog to Machine

Say that my wound is being just a cog in the huge industrial machine, and hardly less so in the front office than on the assembly line. And like a cog I'm robbed of all individuality, stripped of identity, a cipher.

No doubt about the validity of that complaint. Perhaps it is yours.

Again, it becomes a matter of trying to "see" things as they really are.

"Seeing," for example, that the opposite of the cog-making machine is anarchy. What if we could shatter the industrial complex to liberate the cogs, just as the home weavers tried to save their jobs by burning down the newly constructed clothing mills two hundred years ago? Would destroying modern industry liberate us? Could everyone, then, be free? No rules? No bosses? No schedules? A world freed of cogs?

Maybe, but then a world devoid of teamwork, too! No system? No cooperation? But then no industrial production! Civilization robbed of half its content. Yes, the cotton mills did once destroy the home-knitting industries—and then proceeded to clothe the world! Home industries would never have achieved that!

The more complex the economic order becomes, the more and better goods and services it will provide humankind. But the more cogs there will have to be—if the whole is to run most efficiently.

We can't have it two ways; that is, we couldn't enjoy the products of an advanced industrial system if we wanted to do as we pleased on the job. Cars don't get made that way, nor do bathtubs, nor TV sets, nor just about everything else we need to live as well as we do. Anarchy sounds fun, but it fills no storehouses with culture.

True freedom has nothing in common with doing as we please, on the job or anywhere else. Anarchy is not freedom, but license—freedom's counterfeit. When are we "free" to use the highways? When we drive as we please? No, *only* when most drivers maintain order by obeying most of the laws most of the time. Destroy the system so we drive as we please, and, of course, no one would really be free to use the road. Such "freedom" would in fact imprison most of us in our own homes to stay alive.

Freedom and order are twins, inseparable twins. On the road and on the job.

Either each of us must work according to the rules, fitting precisely into the system, or most of our effort will be wasted motion. Doing exactly the tasks assigned us is the only way

45

to share in producing the volume and quality of goods and services that our economy is capable of creating. We are all cogs; some seem to have more "room" than others, but none can perform entirely on their own.

The utter boredom of routines and the mind-numbing monotony of endless repetition is a form of cross-bearing required of many in order that civilization may bless both them and us. For it is as true in the factory, or in the office, or anywhere, as it is on the highways—everyone is most free to draw goods and services from the storehouse of culture when everyone best meets the requirements of orderly participation in the system.

Happily, a genuine cog is a round peg in a round hole, fitted precisely to being what, at that point, the mosaic of culture requires.

There alone resides our freedom to enjoy civilized life.

7

Giving to Receive

The Paycheck

The Bait

And now—that paycheck!

Taking comes easy.

Giving goes hard.

We are likely to *take* the goods and services that come our way from the storehouse of civilization without even considering all the work that has gone into them. We probably think only of the work that we have invested in and getting the paycheck that becomes the key to the storehouse door.

So we never view work as "giving" ourselves to the service of anyone or anything, and we would probably avoid such giving altogether were there no bait to tempt us.

That bait is the paycheck.

We "give" ourselves to our jobs because that's the only way we can earn the money to "buy into" the congealed work of others. The paycheck is the elbow that links the gift of work and the enjoyment of civilization.

That check is both carrot and stick to keep most of us punching in on time year after year. There are the few, the risk takers, out on the cutting edge of vision and progress who are drawn to their work by challenge or driven by ambition or vision without guarantee of reward. However, even they have an eye on the financial returns that work entails.

Money builds a bridge from what we want to what we can buy. Money makes much of the difference between anxiety and security, between hardship and comfort. And so money rules as an idol in many people's lives, so much an idol that St. Paul has to warn us that "the love of money is a root of all kinds of evil" (1 Tim. 6:10).

We lay hands on money via the paycheck.

The brown envelope, the piece of paper within it—these form the goal of each week's work, even after we begin to "see" that work gives meaning to life.

Work, for most of us, is the only way to money. And although the old song has it that "the best things in life are free," almost everyone finds that money is the basic means to our "share" in the civilization that work produces. And while many theorists have proposed ways other than payment for work as the means of distributing keys to the storehouse door, no economy has created a more productive society than that which free market enterprise provides. And so for us, it's that paycheck which baits us into doing the job, like it or not, hate it or not!

Money is an unusual kind of bait, however. A mouse might ignore the cheese in the trap in hopes of dining on something else. The average worker, unlike the mouse, has very limited options: work for whatever bait the job offers ... or feel the pinch pretty soon. It's not quite "work or starve," for most of us, but it is "work or welfare." Not the happiest choice. (We will not enter, here, upon the role of unions as they affect income; important as unionization has been, it does not modify the essentials of our discussion).

We might call it compulsory baiting, these paychecks. If not "like it or lump it," it's "like it or not"—we work anyway!

To enjoy many of the gifts that the work of others provides for us in the storehouse of culture, we have to be working ourselves. We *get* because we *give*! That may not be the first economic law mentioned in textbooks, but it is a fundamental law of work-a-day life. We get the enjoyment of goods and services provided *by* others because we give ourselves to work that provides goods or services *for* others! There is a morality about working that took a long time for me to perceive: We get *because* we give! Odd, really, isn't it? The dog-eat-dog world of economics really runs on a morality it usually pretends to scorn: Why should I give? Who gives me anything? (Think again, friend!)

The paycheck is the "bait" all right—and the "bait" is the key to the storehouse door! And what a fabulous storehouse our form of civilization turns out to be! Before you bad mouth the free-market system, think on that for a while. Other storehouses look bare by comparison.

But Not a Trap

The paycheck follows upon work. Often the harder we work, the larger the paycheck—though, as many workers know, this unfortunately is not an invariable law. That is because, as we shall see, work and wage are not related as cause and effect.

Work does not give our lives meaning by way of the bait!

If the whole of our working got meaning only in the money it earns (though many there be who think so), what meaning would survive once the money was spent?

Meaning is *not* in wage or salary; however, many seek it there.

Granted, of course, we took our first job for the money we could make—no sweat, everyone does. Then we moved to another job, probably to make more money. But how easily it all could become, and for many it did become, the familiar work-to-eat and eat-to-work—that miserable treadmill with but one exit—marked "Retirement or Death"! That's the way it is for all who expect to find life's meaning in spending the money they earn—workers who therefore never seem to earn enough. That's because, of course, the meaning we crave will never be found in the accumulation of things that we buy as wildly as we like.

Of course, we do work "for" money. It's the key to enjoying the fruit of the work of others. *But* we work "at" investing ourselves in goods and services useful to others. It requires constant attention not to lose sight of the difference: *for* money, *at* giving. Work endows life with meaning because of what work *is*, not because of what it earns. Paychecks buy goods and services provided to us through the gift of selves by others, but money buys no meaning. Life's meanings are not for sale!

Work is the great equalizer—everyone has to come to it in order to find meaning in living: no short cuts, no detours, no bargain rates.

Money does oil the wheels on which the world moves, but it is human energy exercised through work that supplies the power. The lubricant is not the dynamic that makes all things go! Money does not create civilization; only work does that! Money spreads civilization around.

We need the bait, but if ever we let the bait become a trap, all the money in the world will not buy our way out.

Fair or Just

To observe what wages are, in themselves, let's ask an ancient question about the relationship between work and wages: What, in your judgment, would be a "fair" wage for your job? Or, if you are a homemaker, what might be a fair wage, if ever you got one, for all that you do?

Or, to put it another and more general way: How does the paycheck relate to your daily work?

Given our choice, most of us workers would no doubt raise our wages or salaries. Everyone would go for improved fringe benefits too.

But how would we justify our claim for more pay as "fair"? Or, if you are presently satisfied with your paycheck, what evidence do you have to show that it is, in fact, what you deserve?

Don't be surprised if you don't know; no one else does, either!

None of the experts has an answer to such questions. No one can "prove" what is a fair wage, nor, for that matter, what is a fair price or honorable profit. Across the centuries of Western history, both moralists and economists have struggled to devise a scientific scale for measuring fairness in both wage and price—with absolutely no success.

Even Karl Marx had a go at it. He was a brilliant mathematician and widely read in economic theory. Rather early in his life, Marx believed that there should be a mathematical formula for calculating exactly what any kind of work is worth. And from that we could determine, he thought, what wages ought to be.

But Marx discovered that he, like everyone before (and after) him, could not come up with the magic code that would scientifically equate work and wage. So he finally concluded that in the perfect, classless society he hoped to see established, work would be required, and rewarded, on the following basis: from each according to his ability, and to each according to his need.

This pleasingly vague formula is in fact a confession that for all his genius Karl Marx could not more precisely define a fair wage or price. Even in that best of worlds of which Marxists dream, no one will know how to measure accurately the worth of work, nor of the goods and services that work produces.

For this reason, it has become the commissar in the Communist society who determines in practice what is meant by Marx's "giving according to ability, and getting according to need." Marxism takes political form in the Communist totalitarian state under which wages and prices are set by bureaucratic and arbitrary authority. This is not, as some Marxists and liberation theologians maintain, only a passing phase in Communist development. The autocratic state is inseparable from the Communist society because wage and price will either be established in the free marketplace or by political fiat—and Communism rejects the free market. Commissars don't intend to, of course, but in fact cannot surrender the heady power a totalitarian economy both gives and requires.

However, if economic theory offers no clue to determining scientifically what is a fair wage or price, how, then, are the wages we earn and the prices we pay defined in the democratic society?

In practice, this is done in the *free* marketplace, where theoretically goods can be sold to the highest bidder, and labor power goes where wage and working conditions attract it. Successful as such economic democracy is by comparison to Communism, the system is always vulnerable to the charge of exposing the weak to exploitation by the ruthless—a matter in which the God of love and justice has a keen concern, as the Bible proclaims.

Why does the fair wage escape mathematical definition?

Because work is essentially a gift, the gift of the self to the service of others—in exchange for the paycheck. And how is a gift to be precisely evaluated? Still more because work is the gift of the worker's *self* to the service of others, and how can the value of such a gift be scientifically calculated? The "laws" of economics trip over gifts and selves. And so in talking about what wage we ought to have, and what prices we ought to pay, we need to move into another language. Not the language of science nor even of exchange but that of morality—the language of the Bible. Economics is an art, rather than a science, and subject to moral rather than mathematical norms.

The right term for evaluating gifts of selves cannot really be "fair" or "unfair" as if that could be calculated in terms of some common, objective standard. It is not a question of "fair" wage or price. We are obliged to talk, as the church long has talked, in terms of *just* or *unjust*. What is the "just" wage and price? This is the terminology of morals, not that of economic science.

The measure of what wage you or I deserve is not really economic nor calculable nor scientific.

The issue in wages (and in prices and profits) is moral, because the basic factors involved are not things but persons, not only quantity but quality, not only the production of goods and services but in these the sculpting of selves. Let's run that through again.…

Conscience and the Double Track

Work and wage run, as it were, on separate, though related, tracks.

Work does not find its meaning in wage. Wage cannot be precisely related to work.

No known scientific calculation will draw the parallel tracks together.

Marxism proposes to force the two tracks into union. The result is the brutality of the totalitarian state, contaminated with the awesome inefficiency of the bureaucrat endowed with power beyond his competence.

In practice, in the democratic society, work and wage are related by the marketplace.

However, the free marketplace can easily turn into the brutal and bitter battleground that engendered Marxism in the first place. To preserve the freedom and avoid the exploitation, another factor must be involved.

That factor is morality, daughter of conscience.

This, then, is where we have come: Work is the gift of self to the service of others that becomes the fabric of civilization. Civilization is the gift of others to the service of ourselves. Wage provides the capacity to buy in on the riches of that civilization. The relationship between work and wage cannot be calculated scientifically and must be governed by the art of creative stewardship guided by moral rather than economic law.

At issue in both work and wage is always justice, both on the job and in the pay envelope—justice to employer in the work done, justice to the employee in the payment rendered. In a broader sense, justice to the employee in wage paid so that there will be market for the goods of civilization; and justice to the employer in the work done, so that the product will be salable and serviceable. The economy that would remain free must consciously choose: either this kind of justice or the ceaseless struggle between capital and labor, which is the only relationship that Marxists think possible between them.

What is a just wage? It is a paycheck that recognizes the personal relationships that underlie work and civilization. Involved are both the needs of the worker—at all levels—and success of the enterprise—in which all are involved. As we will stress in a moment, those whose work is concerned with the creation and administration of wage and price scales must be economic artists whose jobs bear heavy moral responsibility. What the traffic will bear or wage scales that only grim necessity will oblige the poor to accept are artistic guidelines that enjoy no endorsement from heaven. The search for just wage and fair price is never-ending, for the market is always changing and so are the forms required of work.

Economic justice is by no means universal even in the best of civilizations.

A migrant worker and his family may work very hard, on very long days, to bring in less than some white-collar worker may pick up in an hour.

Because there is no scientific formula for calculating the just wage, no one can "prove" that the migrant is underpaid or that the high-salaried executive gets "too much."

However, the Lord employs recession and revolution to warn that when some wages are too low and some incomes far exceed just desert, conscience is violated and God whose bounties underlie the economy is shortchanged.

The moral aspect to our daily work concerns how well the job is being done for which we are accepting our paychecks. How creatively have we developed our talents? How enthusiastically do we attack new challenges? How eagerly do we accept responsibilities? What is the "ratio" of excellence between our God-given gifts and work-produced goods and services? It is here that sheep divide from goats—both in the shop and in the board room or executive suite. The morality of the just wage corresponds to the morality of honest work—for everyone!

Work and wage move, then, on parallel tracks. There can be a close proximity between them, as when more and better work is rewarded with higher income. But neither track is the cause of the other or the goal of the other. The track representing work provides all the goods and services that together create civilized life. The track representing wage leads to the workers' own enjoyment of the fruits of the world's work.

Without the labor track, no civilization.

Without the wages track, no one to buy in, and hence nothing sold—and, again, no civilization.

Conscience relates the two tracks by way of executive stewardship, to which we turn next.

8

THE END OF THE MATTER

Executive Stewardship

Executive Stewardship

Work and wage draw together at the point where conscience functions, that is to say, work and wage tracks coalesce in persons making executive decisions.

That's what an executive is: one who makes decisions. Strictly speaking, the good executive only executes the will of others, be it management in general or the board of directors.

Stewardship?

That's the overall term for how we choose to use, moment by moment, all that God places on loan to us, for precisely the purpose of testing the sculpting power of our *executive stewardship*.

All of us, of course, are just such executives, with God's will as the mandate given us to execute.

All of us, too, are just such stewards, for we each carry about within us God's investment of life, time, and talent.

All work, we have been saying, is alike, not in form or content but in essence. Whatever work we do puts our selves into the service of others and at the same time sculpts the kind of self each is becoming. No matter what our work is.

But certain jobs unite work and wage (and price) in someone's decision. Some workers have been given talents that push them to the top, as we are likely to view it, of the economic structure. They have the awesome obligation of setting wage and price scales for employees and products. Theirs is the gift for merging all economic variables into price tags and wage rates—and their choices are as sculpting of their own selves as any others. Conscience sets before these executive stewards an ideal free-economy goal of (1) the best product; (2) produced under the best working conditions for all employees, including themselves; (3) at the best wage for everyone involved; and (4) reflecting the best efforts at every job, to be sold at the lowest price compatible with these requirements.

We have said that the twin tracks of work and wage do not meet, and cannot be scientifically related. They are bridged by morality, not by mathematics. And it is in the self-sculpting choices of wage and price scales that managers must make the twin tracks merge—under the all-seeing eye of God. It is here that justice, as defined by the will of the Creator and revealed in his Word, comes to bear upon the economy.

The executive who seeks to avoid responsibility for his choices by seeming to let the market, or what the traffic will bear, or what necessity will oblige employees to accept become his conscience is in fact putting his choices in the service of idols—and idolatry is no more acceptable to God in board rooms and executive suites than it is in the shadowed temples of paganism. Setting wages and prices, while keeping an industry or business sound and healthy, is far from easy. Failures occur. But conscience sets before managerial executives the goal of the ideal sketched above, challenging them to make their wage and price decisions with an eye fixed on justice. Such decisions sculpt selves destined for beatitude.

Executive stewardship involves us all, of course.

Have we always envied "big" names? Always wanted to be responsible for really important decisions?

Well, we are. Each of us is! Upon our decisions hangs the destiny of a human self—our own self—of more importance Jesus says than the whole world besides.

Have we always wanted to be noticed, to be watched by important people, to "play" before a really significant audience?

Well, we do. Each of us does!

We live our lives, inside and out, in the omnipresence of God! We "play" every moment before an Audience of One—who holds our destiny in his hand! Aware of that, we should live our lives as wholly unto him, every moment!

It all comes down, day by day, moment by moment to executive decision!

Ultimate Return

God is the world's primary investor. He takes the initial risk of putting life, time, and talent at the disposal of each of us.

Like all prudent investors, the Lord God is in search of return upon his capital. What "interest" does this primary investor seek on the life, time, and talent which he commits to each of us?

The final return God wants is the most precious possession any of us has—the self!

God wants the *self*—yours, mine, everyone's!

He wants each of us, then, as sheep. For only sheep spend eternity in the presence of God.

Everything comes down to this, finally: Does he get or lose you? And each of us? Sheep or goat? Do we love him first (becoming his sheep) or ourselves first (becoming goat)? What does our behavior say?

That is not only most important to God. It is, of course, of eternal importance to each of us.

All the agonies of history root in this: God leaves man free to choose between sculpting himself sheep or goat. Why does God run and oblige us to run this incalculable risk? Because a freely given love is the only kind of true love there is. God loves us freely, certainly without merit of it on our part; God chooses to risk losing us in order to receive freely our love (that is our willing obedience) in return. That is the "interest" the investing God is after.

The only immortal possession we shall ever have is ... our selves!

All else entrusted to our care, all else we could possibly assemble in the way of goods of every kind, is as nothing in comparison to what the Bible calls the "soul"—the selves we are sculpting every day!

We do a great deal of that sculpting every day on the job.

That's why working gives meaning to living!

That's the way it is, at whatever the level—by human standards—of the work we do, be it at the "top" or at the "bottom" of the ladder.

It's not, finally, on what rung of that ladder we are working.

It's all in the "love"—that is will to obey in which each of us does his job.

For that aim will determine what happens to the most precious possession entrusted to the care of each of us: the final destiny of each *self*!

Theological Note

Just one theological observation for those interested in such things: The theme of this essay is not derived from a theology of "works righteousness" nor based on the assumption that salvation can be earned by our selves. God's gifts of life, time, and talent flower in his ultimate gift: redemption in Jesus Christ to all who receive him in faith. By faith we are liberated in Christ from inherited bondage to the Devil; by faith we are restored to the spiritual liberty that enables us to draw from the Spirit strength to choose the obedience that sculpts sheep. All obedience is by faith, lived in divine grace. My thesis is simply that of St. Paul, the great apostle of faith: "work out your salvation with fear and trembling ..." (Phil. 2:12).

In short, we are indeed "saved" by faith, but faith without the works that sculpt sheep is a nonfaith; it is "dead" (James 2:26).

And Now

And now, we can say some things about work—your work, my work, and everyone's—which might have seemed strange at the beginning of our discussion.

Consider such things as the following:

1. Work is Everyman's artistry, a kind of poetry of the world, for through it is woven the delicate and balanced rhythmic structure of culture and civilization. Work is Everyman as artist. For through our work each of us not only fashions goods and services pleasing to another, but each in the same process sculpts himself, or herself, into the ultimate destiny we are really seeking. Work makes an artist's studio out of shop, kitchen, office, wherever ...

2. Work *liberates*: because work frees its product from dispersion in a miscellany of raw materials just as the artistry of the sculptor frees his statue from the cold embrace of marble.

3. Work *molds*: a wilderness into a garden, nature into a city. Human history begins in the Garden of Eden, and culminates in the New Jerusalem; man's history wends its way from one to the other on the bent backs, active minds, vivid imaginations, and straining sinews of human labor.

4. Work *mediates*: between a field and a harvest, between a harvest and human nourishment. Work unites fibers into cloth, and transforms trees into homes. Work flies the skies,

defies the darkness, explores the moon and the planets. Work is the storehouse of today's riches and tomorrow's secrets.

5. Work, said Marx, "is the language of real life." Those who escape work avoid using that language and therefore confuse merely existing with truly living.

6. Work is the mystery that provides us with far more than we could ever provide ourselves.

7. Work gives an idea a time and place. Work endows vision with reality and hope with substance.

8. Work exerts the discipline of nature upon the development of the worker's self—steel will not be treated like plastic or wood like liquid. Through work, man obeys nature's laws and thus transforms nature into his servant and himself into a work of art.

9. Work joins man with God in the development of the universe. And this leads us to a final perspective from which to "see" work—our own *work*—as it really is. We can put that perspective in a sentence:

> ***Work is the form in which we make ourselves
> useful to man and thus to God!***

Afterword

Made for Hope

Greg Forster

One day two things dawned on me: (1) If life is to have meaning, I would have to find it, not hope to create it for myself. (2) Living must get its meaning, first of all, on the job, because that's the drain down which the best hours of every week dribble away.

At first, these options seemed fanciful: Life's meaning on the job? Not because I put it there, but because *work* endows living with significance? Kidding somebody?

No kidding at all. That's the way it is.

—Lester DeKoster,
Work: The Meaning of Your Life, xiv

When they first hear the message of the faith and work movement, a lot of people roll their eyes. *Made for work?* they think. *That's a nice theory. You should try doing my job.*

This is a deep problem for the faith and work movement. A recent Gallup survey found that 70 percent of American workers feel disengaged at work, or outright hate their jobs.[1]

---

1. "State of the American Workplace," Gallup Inc., June 11, 2013.

That's on top of ten million people who want to work but are unemployed, and the steadily increasing number of people—now fully 30 percent of adult men—who aren't even looking for work.[2] Our culture isn't always well prepared to hear that work is a great and glorious thing.

The world of work is also changing rapidly. New technologies and the global economy continue to reshape who does what, how they do it, what they get paid for it, and just about every other structural aspect of our work. Because we know that the world of work is broken, the rapid pace of change can be frightening. Where can we turn for security? Is there a moral order in our work that doesn't change, even though all its conditions seem to be subject to almost limitless innovation? Will technological advances and global competition dehumanize us, reducing the worker to just another cog in the machine?

In this essay, we will look at how one author dealt with these problems by putting the Christian virtue of hope front and center. Lester DeKoster wrote his profound little book *Work: The Meaning of Your Life* for factory workers who felt utterly degraded and demoralized by their work. His message of hope to them is an outstanding model for our movement today. And his deep thinking about work points us away from superficial approaches to a fully three-dimensional model of what it means to work.

Does Good Really Run Deeper than Evil?

Work is broken for all of us, because we and our world are broken. We feel that brokenness in our work every day. It's toilsome. It's frustrating. A lot of the time, we feel more like the work is doing us than we are doing it. On top of that,

2. "The Employment Situation—May 2014," U.S. Bureau of Labor Statistics, June 6, 2014; Nicholas Eberstadt, "The Astonishing Collapse of Work in America," Real Clear Markets, July 10, 2013.

coworkers can be hostile, manipulative, even dishonest. And all our hard work can fall apart and come to nothing, even if we do everything right, because of forces outside our control.

Theologically, it is critically important to keep our affirmation of the goodness of work front and center. God's activity in creation and redemption must always be seen as more powerful and more important—more *ultimate*—than our brokenness and the brokenness of our world. Good runs deeper than evil in this universe, and talking as though evil ran just as deep as good is not just a mistake. It is damnable heresy.

And yet, paradoxically, if we start with God's goodness and how we can find it in our work, many people struggle to connect that to their daily experience in any tangible way. There are some who can do so, by God's grace. But many find little connection between the theoretical affirmation of God's goodness and their practical experience of toil and frustration—of the enormity of evil and the curse, dragging us down day after day.

Thus we seem to be locked in a trap. If we talk about work as a place of goodness and light, where God is present and active, for many this seems to have little daily relevance. But if we talk about work as a place of darkness and curse, we risk losing the gospel itself. For the gospel says that God really is, in fact, the only ultimate ruler of this universe, and he really has, in fact, defeated evil and swallowed up the darkness in his glorious light.

Hope is the key that opens this lock. It is the only sword that can cut this Gordian knot. With our eyes, we often see a world dominated by evil and curse. But we are to live by faith, not by sight (2 Cor. 5:7). And what is this faith that is so powerful we can live by it even in defiance of our own sight? It is the assurance of what we hope for (Heb. 11:1).

The art of helping people live out their faith in their work is largely the art of *giving them something to hope for*. It is the art of helping them become aware of the larger realities that define the deepest meaning of their work. Their eyes don't see these larger realities on a daily basis; our job is to help them remember these things when their eyes don't see them.

Crucially, the "larger realities" people need to remember include more than just the spiritual realities that eyes can never see. They also include a lot of plain, humdrum facts in the material world that we don't see every day simply because we don't happen to bump into them. In their work, people must not only know Christ (who is not seen because he is present by the Spirit). They must also know the millions of neighbors their work is serving (who are not seen because they are physically remote from the workplace). It is this broader sight, both of spiritual realities and of material realities that are physically remote, that makes hope possible.

This brings us to Lester DeKoster and his powerful little book.

Only Hopeful Work Can Build a Meaningful Life

DeKoster, a professor at Calvin College, gave speech classes in the evenings for blue-collar workers in his city. He heard most of them describe their daily lives at work as meaningless and degrading. They felt like they were nobody, like they were slaves, like they were just part of the machinery on the shop floor, like no one cared about them as human beings. They saw no dignity or meaning in what they did.

DeKoster knew that this darkness, large as it might loom in their sight, was not the deepest truth about their work. So in 1982 he wrote them—and all other workers who labor in the darkness—a book: *Work: The Meaning of Your Life.*

Interpreting their experiences in the light of the parables of Matthew 25, DeKoster lays out a simple but powerful framework for connecting work to both gospel hope and the structures of human civilization. At sixty-two pages, it is a beautiful gift that continues to give to the church today.

DeKoster argues that we must bring hope to our work if we are to have hope at all. Our view of work shapes our lives more than anything else, simply because we spend more time working than doing anything else. Work is not all of life, but it is central to how we find meaning, purpose, and dignity in our existence—or fail to find it.

Those who don't find transcendent meaning in their work live as though their existence is mostly meaningless. Their character and life choices are shaped accordingly. Even if they are Christians, if they don't connect their faith to their work, they will be what Doug Spada and Dave Scott call "Monday Morning Atheists," living the bulk of their lives *as though* they are without God and without hope in the world. Their faith, while real, remains confined within the bounds of what Mark Greene calls "leisure-time Christianity."

DeKoster writes that for people who don't find meaning in work, whether Christian or not, human life is essentially "a wilderness of work." Each day is a desert of meaningless toil that we have to trudge through, day after day. Our burning thirst for significance is quenched only occasionally—and briefly—by the "oases of meaning furnished by our families, the church, politics, community affairs, plus hobbies and spectator sports thrown in to give zest to leisure" (xiii).

The remedy to this bleak existence, DeKoster argues, comes when "a right view of work becomes the key to a satisfying life" (xv). If we live out a God-centered approach to work, we will be grounding the bulk of our lives squarely in God. Our spiritual longings will be satisfied.

Moreover, DeKoster boldly asserts that "if work can give a central core of meaning to living, then all other meanings cluster around this one" (xv). Though we might yearn for a different kind of life—one in which work is peripheral—that's just not the way we're wired. God has *designed* us to spend most of our lives working.

So for DeKoster, bringing hope to the world of work is not only crucial to finding meaning in our work, but to finding meaning in our lives as a whole. If we do our daily work without the hope that God is present and active in it, our lives become "a wilderness of work," a desert through which we trudge, desperately thirsting for meaning and purpose. If we work with hope, that desperate thirst will be satisfied—not only in our work, but increasingly in the rest of our lives as well.

Our Beloved Hope: To Work Is to Love God by Loving Your Neighbors

Why did God design us to spend most of our time working? "This is really the open secret of all that follows," writes DeKoster at the start of the book: "Work is the form in which we make ourselves useful to others.... That is why work gives meaning to life" (1).

We can work with hope because *to do good work is to love your neighbor*. Our work, whether paid or unpaid, skilled or unskilled, glamorous or unnoticed, serves human needs. It is by working, and only by working, that we are able to provide people with what they require to survive and thrive.

DeKoster asks us to imagine what would happen if those factory workers in his speech classes stopped working:

> Food vanishes from the store shelves, gas pumps dry up, streets are no longer patrolled, and fires burn themselves out. Communication and transportation services end and utilities go dead. Those who survive at all are soon huddled around campfires, sleeping in tents, and clothed in rags. The difference between barbarism and culture is, simply, work. (2–3)

Just imagine what this new perspective on their work must have been like for those factory workers DeKoster was teaching. Your work has dignity and meaning, even in the face of all brokenness, because the survival of civilization itself depends on you! This is what it means to love your neighbor.

The impact our work has on our communities is one of those "larger realities" that define the meaning of our work. We don't see it with our eyes every day, and if we lose our awareness of it, we lose the ability to do our work as a full expression of love for neighbor. Hence we must constantly draw the eyes of our souls back, and back again, to the larger world that the eyes of our bodies can't see. (Pastors, take note—this is a lot easier if someone else prompts us to do it!)

However, work by itself is not enough. *Love for neighbor* by itself is not enough. Christians know that God is at the center of all, and must be at the center of our own lives. So if DeKoster is right that work is central to the meaning of our lives, where is God in our work?

God is present with us in and through our work, no matter how broken it is. God has put "making ourselves useful to others" at the center of life's meaning for two reasons: "First, God himself chooses to be served through the work that serves others.… Second, God has so made us that through working we actually sculpt the kind of selves we each are becoming, in time and for eternity" (9).

To illustrate this twofold presence of God in our work, DeKoster turns to two familiar parables from Matthew 25: the Parable of the Talents (vv. 14–30) and the Parable of the Sheep and the Goats (vv. 31–46). At first, we might be tempted to focus on how "God is served by our work" in the Parable of the Talents, and how "our work shapes ourselves for God" in the Parable of the Sheep and the Goats. However, DeKoster shows that each of these themes is actually present in both parables.

Our Decisive Hope: Serving God and Shaping Self in the Parable of the Sheep and the Goats

DeKoster writes that for many years, he interpreted the Parable of the Sheep and the Goats as a call to support special programs and do religious works. Now, however, his thinking has changed:

> Once it seemed to commend special acts of giving, such as charities that we ought to be doing in our spare time.... But it now seems to me that Jesus is obviously speaking of more than a vocational behavior or pastime kindnesses. Why? Because he hinges our entire eternal destiny upon giving ourselves to the service of others—and that can hardly be a pastime event. In fact, giving ourselves to the services of others, as obviously required by the Lord, is precisely what the central block of life that we give to working turns out to be! (11)

The first of DeKoster's two modes of God's presence in our work—that God is served by it—is explicitly emphasized in the parable:

> I was hungry and you gave me something to eat.
>
> The Lord is saying that where humans are hungry, there he too chooses to hunger. He waits in the hungry man or woman or child, longing to be served. Served how? By the work of those who knit the garment of civilization through the production and distribution of food! (13)

Underneath this heading, DeKoster provides a lengthy list of occupations whose daily work is dedicated to feeding the hungry:

- Farmers, ranchers, and other agricultural workers
- Bakers, chefs, and other culinary workers

- Truckers, packers, and other transportation workers
- Wholesalers, retailers, and other commercial workers
- Kitchen and restaurant staff, and other hospitality workers
- All those who produce the tools and support services these professions need

… and so forth. The list is impressively long. When the roll is fully called, millions of people will be able to hear their daily work praised in the words, "I was hungry and you fed me."

DeKoster then goes down the list from the parable—"I was thirsty…. I needed clothes…. I was sick…. I was a stranger…. I was in prison…."—and provides for each one a long list of occupations whose daily work is dedicated to meeting that need. It is all of us, through our daily work, who carry out these tasks. We can all work with hope because we are all serving Christ when we serve our neighbors' needs!

But don't the lost, or the "goats" of the parable, do this kind of work as well? Why wouldn't an unbelieving farmer or kitchen worker hear the same benediction, "I was hungry and you gave me something to eat"? That question brings us to the second mode of God's presence in our work—that it shapes ourselves for him.

What matters most to God is not that you go through the motions of doing work, but how and why you do it. In fact, the very reason it matters so much to God *whether* you work is because he cares so much about how and why you work!

In the parable, the saved and the lost are represented not simply as people with different track records, but as two different types of people. In real life, the difference between a sheep and a goat is not so much that they do different things as that they are different things. Similarly, DeKoster argues, the point of the parable is that God's people are different in kind from others.

The Son of Man pronounces his judgment simply by revealing to people what they truly are:

> The sheep got to the throne as already sheep; the goats got to the throne as already goats…. The parable is teaching us that we will "see" at last what day-to-day living is all about. (12)

> In the end, both sheep and goats are simply guided to the place they have been seeking all their lives: sheep are led to the company of the Lord they served, perhaps unknowingly; goats are assigned the place where goats could alone belong—among their kind, in the alienation from each other and from God that they practiced in life. (19)

DeKoster is reading the parable as a reflection on sanctification. Those who spend their lives serving God in their daily work will become, more and more, the kind of people who belong in God's sheepfold. They will develop a certain kind of character, Christian virtues, and spiritual formation. Meanwhile, those who spend their lives serving themselves will become, more and more, the kind of people who would find no place in God's sheepfold. Their sinful nature is given greater and greater expression in their lives, and is thus imprinted deeper and deeper in their characters.[3]

---

3. Unfortunately, as he focuses on sanctification, DeKoster is not always careful to keep in view the doctrines of regeneration and justification by faith apart from the works of the law. God's "sheep" do become more and more sheep-like over the course of their lives by doing the work of sheep. But it was not that kind of work, or any kind of work of their own, that made them sheep in the first place. They were born as goats, and it took a miracle of God to make them sheep. Moreover, the track record of good works that earns their place in heaven is not theirs, but Christ's. DeKoster knew all this, and near the end of the book

Our Fruitful Hope: Serving God and Shaping Self in the Parable of the Talents

The Parable of the Talents is one of the classic texts for contemplating the meaning of our daily work. However, many expositions of the parable don't get far beyond saying that God calls on us to work and attributes eternal significance to how well we answer that call. DeKoster uses the theme of God's twofold presence in our work to uncover some deeper layers of the parable.

DeKoster reminds us that the divine calling to work implies God himself is served by our work, and draws our attention to the democratizing, equalizing effect of this fact:

> The Master's intent is obvious: service. That is why each of the recipients of his largesse is called a *servant*.... Notice, too, that the eye of heaven sees work in its essence and takes small account of differences among jobs that we think are very important. Five-talent people look very "successful" by all worldly standards, stirring their pride and our envy; one-talent people risk our contempt and their own despair. But in the Master's eye "ratio" levels us all.... No ground for pride; no excuse for envy. (24–25)

The modern economy, which creates large differences in financial rewards for different kinds of work, cannot be sustained culturally without this sense of equal dignity among "five-talent" and "one-talent" workers. The pride of the five-talenter and the envy of the one-talenter create social conflict

---

he inserts what he calls a "Theological Note" to clarify that he has no intention of downplaying the Protestant understanding of regeneration and justification (60–61). Still, it would have been preferable if he had touched on these themes more often, to keep the relationship between justification and sanctification more clear.

that eventually becomes unsustainable—unless a spiritual influence works to mitigate that pride and envy.

The shaping of the self for God is also present in the parable. DeKoster shows how it illuminates the strict work ethic of the New Testament ("If anyone is not willing to work, let him not eat," 2 Thess. 3:10). Sloth is a sin because work is divine activity:

> The faithful servant is expected to work, you noticed, at full capacity. That, then, is the ratio that God blesses— *full* use of whatever talents we are given. Five-talent people are required to turn in a five-talent performance; so also with the two-talent folk, and so on. His is the choice as to our talents; ours is the duty to use them to the fullest. (24)

Here, again, the biblical view of work is a democratizing and equalizing force. DeKoster emphasizes that there is no important distinction between the sloth of the rich man living off his wealth; the sloth of the middle-class slacker who puts in the minimum effort needed to get by; and the sloth of the poor man who finds panhandling or welfare more comfortable than a job. "On all such loafers, and any others, God takes a grim stand," DeKoster writes (26).

But this biblical work ethic is no mere pharisaical, legalistic condemnation of sloth. In the opening passage of this chapter, DeKoster provides his clearest and most powerful statement on how work "shapes the self" for God on a daily basis:

> The chisel we use to sculpt our selves is choice. It's not a chisel of our own making; it's a tool we can't avoid using. To live is to choose—even when we decline to choose, that is itself a choice…. Do we choose what to think, what to say, what to do in obedience to our Creator's will? Or, do we choose in obedience to self, or to any of the many other beguiling disguises worn by the Devil? We are always in the service of some

"master"—ultimately, in the service of God or his Adversary. Obedience to God's will sculpts sheep, while rebellion molds goats.

And because work looms so large in a lifetime, the choices we make on the job play a decisive role in what kind of selves we are becoming. How do we sculpt our selves on the job? We do it with the chisel of choice, day by day. How well do we choose to do the work at hand? How well do we choose to develop and to use the talents God has given us? What is the quantity and quality of the work we choose to turn out, every hour? How do we choose—as employer or as employee—to relate to others on the job? (22)

Work is a crucible of character—a place where we become more and more the kind of people we already are in our hearts. That's why slothfulness is such serious business: it's a refusal to shape our selves for God. DeKoster explains, "Work is a duty. Why? Because God loans talents for the purpose of reaping return. Or, to put it another way: God loans us talents to enable us to choose the kind of self we will sculpt through using them" (27).

Our Steadfast Hope: Bearing the Cross for God's Glory

Don't get the wrong impression. For all this talk about how God is present with us in and through our work, DeKoster has not forgotten to connect with the brokenness and frustration of his audience. One of the great strengths of *Work* is the vivid portrait it paints of the toil and sorrow of daily work, and the message of hope and perseverance it brings to that world.

DeKoster devotes an entire chapter of his book to recording what he heard from those factory workers in his speech classes. "I have had some tutors of my own on the dark side of the job.... What a collection I might also compile of stories of blasted hopes and maimed spirits as recounted in sometimes halting tones from the speech platform" (29–30). He is careful to note that all people's work is broken, not just that of factory line workers (30). On the other hand, in light of our special duties to the poor and the marginalized, the challenges of the line worker are a worthy focus of attention.

A striking theme that emerges from DeKoster's account of the factory workers' lamentations is something that goes beyond merely the pain and frustration of the daily burdens they bear. These workers want to know whether anyone cares. More painful than the physical and emotional strain are the deeper questions of meaning and relationship. Does it matter that I bear this? And does anyone care that I do?

Deep in their hearts, hurting and broken people want spiritual comfort—hope—more than they want material comfort. And that's a good thing, because according to Christianity they actually need spiritual comfort much more than they need material comfort. The good news is, while material comfort is always expensive and often unattainable, spiritual comfort is available to all. It is a free gift for those who turn themselves over to God.

But while hope is free, it is not easy. DeKoster's starting point for bringing hope to broken work is the cross. "Christianity long ago took full account of the wounds we may suffer at work. 'If anyone would come after me, he must deny himself and take up his cross daily and follow me' (Luke 9:23)" (35). Just as Jesus gave himself up to be broken, we must give ourselves up to be broken.

The answer to the broken worker's cry, "does anybody care?" is a resounding yes! Yes, God cares, cares immeasurably, for the worker who keeps showing up faithfully to the toilsome, frustrating job that serves his community and keeps civilization running. When we take up our cross daily and bear it in our work, we please God.

This yes contains one of the most important fulfillments of God's promises of hope. Christian hope is not only for the eschaton; while the final consummation of hope is in the future, the firstfruits of hope are already present with us. To please God gives us dignity and meaning even in the midst of the most broken situations.

DeKoster connects cross-bearing—perseverance under trial—to his earlier themes of work serving others and shaping the self. In one of the most moving passages in the book, DeKoster asks us to consider how the persevering workers of his world must look from God's perspective:

> As the Lord surveys his world, what a host of rugged heroes and heroines of labor he must behold! Those who rise with the sun, lifelong, to jobs that demand endless self-sacrifice, and get in return but little reward in pay and still less in recognition. Those who see no sunshine all the day long, in the caverns of the earth or the noisome dungeons of heavy industry. And those— no less heroic—who find their substantial salary and bonuses but small recompense for the burdens, and the envy, their "success" involves. Those who must day by day drive weary bodies and spent minds to one more effort. Those who wrestle with bureaucracy to keep businesses solvent long after patience and pleasure are dead. Some who exercise initiative without appreciation, but persevere well beyond the need for personal monetary reward. Mothers whose lives are poured into their families; fathers whose bodies are sacrificed that their wives and children might live. God sees migrant families struggling hopelessly from dawn to dusk; peasants who grub like slaves without hope; service employees called any time for emergencies, surrendering their family holidays or busy through the dark of night.
>
> "Lose your life …," is Jesus asking us [Luke 9:24]? He is talking about the martyrdoms of labor, too. (37)

It is the shaping of ourselves in this perseverance that earns the Lord's "well done" in the Parable of the Talents, the benediction that provides our lives with the only eternal meaning and purpose they can ultimately have. And it is the weaving of civilization from the threads of our work, as we serve one another's needs, that grounds the Lord's "you did it unto me" in the Parable of the Sheep and the Goats. The fallen world is a world of hunger, sickness, and strangers; our work feeds, heals, and welcomes our fellow human beings in need. Hope is not just for individuals seeking dignity and meaning; it is for communities seeking to flourish.

Our Unchanging Hope: The Two-Edged Swords of Technology and Globalization

The continuing advance of technology is one of the most important factors shaping work in the modern world. It enables us to serve human needs far more effectively, lifting millions around the world out of poverty, hunger, disease, and death. At the same time, technology's power to reshape our work can have bad effects as well as good ones. Ever since the emergence of the modern factory in the eighteenth century, some observers have worried that the conditions of work in modernity must inevitably be unnatural and inhumane. Technology has also brought about the globalization of markets, extending economic relationships to the point where almost everyone in the world can do business with one another. This, too, has produced many benefits and many anxieties.

DeKoster took a keen interest in these subjects, partly because they were so critically important to the challenges facing the factory workers in his classes. His approach is a strange mix of optimism and pessimism. On both sides of that ledger he has important things to say. Yet his optimism is sometimes too optimistic, and his pessimism is sometimes too pessimistic.

When he contemplates the good that is, and can be, accomplished by technology and globalization, he is effusive:

> It's simply far better to be one of the workers tending the needs of a huge mechanical harvester as part of some vast agribusiness than to live in a world where starvation stalks its millions of victims. Technology makes it possible to produce enough food now around the world to feed everyone.... Technology has revolutionized civilization, and it promises untold achievements ahead! The work that serves it weaves the fabric of culture. (43–44)

The benefits are more than just material; they are spiritual. True, millions of people around the world get to not starve to death as a result of economic and technological progress. More important, however, is the fact that we are now in meaningful relationship with them through economic exchange. "Work ranges far ahead of politics in bringing the peoples of the globe closer together. The multinational corporations ... draw diverse sinews of labor into cooperative and constructive effort which transcends geographic boundaries, penetrates political borders, and even joins East and West, North and South" (39).

Paradoxically, at the same time he is offering these optimistic encouragements, DeKoster seems to agree with the critics who think technology makes the conditions of work less humane. He argues that this is the price we must pay for the blessings that technology allows us to create for our fellow human beings. He offers no assurances that as progress continues, this price will not end up being quite high. "Those who 'pay' for technological achievements by serving the robots give just that much more of themselves to cross-bearing for human progress" (44). He bluntly tells us, in effect, to suck it up and pay the price, for our neighbors' sake as well as our own.

There is much value in DeKoster's perspective on technological change. On the optimistic side, new technologies and global markets do give us a breathtaking, unprecedented power to love our neighbors and contribute to worldwide human flourishing. From 1970 to 2006, the portion of the world population living on a dollar per day or less dropped 80 percent. Literally a billion people rose up out of that level of extreme poverty. Living standards have doubled globally.[4] More importantly, this progress has been achieved in part through an unprecedented expansion of respect for human rights and the building of relationships between cultures.[5]

The overall biblical narrative does give us good grounds for hope that technological advancement is not intrinsically evil or disordering. Nature was given to humanity in the beginning so that our work could transform it for the better. That is what we are seeing today as billions around the world emerge from poverty, thanks to technology and globalization.

DeKoster's realism about technological change also gives us good food for thought. It is healthy to be reminded that we can't have it all. DeKoster is right when he says that even if technological advancement has some downsides, the alternative is mass starvation and barbarism. Are we prepared to condemn millions of people in Africa, India, and China to die so we can have the luxury of pursuing our romantic visions of traditional agricultural life?

And yet, DeKoster's optimism sometimes carries him too far. At one point in the book, he even seems to be offering overconfident promises of global peace and prosperity (39–40). We need not go that far! Hope is a Christian virtue,

---

4. Maxim Pinkovskiy and Xavier Sala-i-Martin, "Parametric Estimations of the World Distribution of Income," National Bureau of Economic Research, October 2009.

5. See Wayne Grudem and Barry Asmus, *The Poverty of Nations* (Wheaton, IL: Crossway, 2013).

but not naïveté about the brokenness of the world. While the potential of technology and globalization is very great, it is a two-edged potential. God never owes us success.[6]

We also need not fully accept DeKoster's flat, suck-it-up pessimism about dehumanized work environments. Here, for once, he is insufficiently hopeful. A robust Christian hope, no matter how tempered by realism, does not leave room for simply accepting the dominion of brokenness. Even common sense will tell us that an economic order built exclusively on cross-bearing will be unsustainable in the long run.

However, more than just a deficiency of hope is at work. DeKoster's views are shaped by the books of economic and sociological scholars—Adam Smith, Karl Marx, Max Weber, and their scholarly successors—who did not accurately keep track of the real empirical effects of technological change. While the initial disruptions of traditional agricultural life in the eighteenth century created many inhumane work practices, over time technology has tended to make the conditions of work more humane rather than less so.

In a fallen world that is under the curse of Genesis 3:17–19, the most "natural" condition of work is back-breaking, highly repetitive field labor, starting in early childhood and continuing without interruption until death. Industrialization has not, overall, made working conditions worse. In the long run it has made them much better—much more humane.

So while some people in some situations may be called to the kind of extraordinary sacrifice DeKoster describes, this need not be the normal situation. The working population

---

6. It is possible DeKoster's overly optimistic expectations for global peace and prosperity are influenced by postmillennial eschatology. If so, those of us who don't take the postmillennial view would do well to make charitable allowances for theological differences before judging him too harshly. But we can still, with charity, decline to join him in his more effusive predictions.

in general should not give up its humanity, even to feed the world—and at this point all indications are that no such sacrifice will, in fact, be demanded. In the eighteenth century, pastoral leaders like John Wesley embraced the Industrial Revolution and affirmed the legitimacy of the modern, entrepreneurial economy that was emerging. But they also fought to reform practices like child labor or workplaces that were unsafe or unsanitary. We can do the same, embracing technology and globalization for their benefits without turning our consciences over to them.

Our Shared Hope: Community, Freedom, and Responsibility in the Social Order

"The end of the matter," DeKoster writes, is "executive stewardship." God has made human beings—both as individuals and collectively in communities—to manage and cultivate the creation order. By the word *executive*, he stresses the role of human mind, will, and conscience. "That's what an executive is: one who makes decisions" (57). We are thinking and choosing creatures, morally responsible for our actions, and this mysterious agency and responsibility is central to who we are as image-bearers. By the word *stewardship*, he stresses that our agency is made to be used in service to God, for his glory. We do make decisions as the world's resident executives, but "the good executive only executes the will of others" (57).

Executive stewardship raises the final big question DeKoster takes on in *Work*—the nature of community. In the final sections of the book, he turns from the task of encouraging individual workers to see their work as part of a larger social whole, and takes up the nature of the whole itself. We are all, individually, executive stewards. But we are also members of a community, and to do our work well we must begin with that in mind. So what does a community of executive stewards look like?

This question would seem to present us with an unsolvable problem. If each individual is an executive, pursuing his or her own personal vision of stewardship, how can all our work fit together and weave a civilization? But if we take away that personal agency and authority from the worker, haven't we stripped the individual of his or her status as an executive steward? How do we respect the image of God in each individual while holding the community together?

These questions are no less pressing today than they were in 1982. Granted, the context has changed; DeKoster encountered these questions in part through the Cold War confrontation between capitalism and communism. This background should be borne in mind when reading DeKoster, because it shaped some of his analysis—as was the case in virtually all writing on the topic of work in the Cold War era.

But DeKoster also encountered these questions through the sense of powerlessness and loss of identity he met in those factory workers. *That* context has not changed much. It demanded an answer then, and still demands one today. Even the larger social and historical questions that shaped the Cold War—can a nation be free and have community at the same time?—remain relevant for members of our communities today.

Work ought to have a context of freedom. Only if work is done freely can it fully express love for neighbor, and shape us into the kind of people God wants us to be. "Freedom" does not mean anarchism or libertarianism. It means treating people as executive stewards, as stewards over all that rightfully lies within their sphere of control and influence—which is exactly what God says they are.

At the most immediate level, the executive stewardship of the individual and the needs of the community meet through economic exchange. Each of us does his or her job, providing for the needs of others. Each of us gets paid for this work, and we use the wages to acquire the goods and services created by other people's work.

This exchange also requires a context of freedom if it is to be done in love. As DeKoster profoundly puts it, "work and wage draw together at the point where conscience functions" (57). Work is inextricably linked with economic exchange, and conscience sits atop the connection governing both. But only if we are given freedom to live as executive stewards can our daily work and wage fully provide the opportunity for conscience to function effectively.

How, then, can free people have community? The starting point of the answer is that *work and exchange create community by creating harmony and peace*. Work heals broken relationships and forges a shared sense of identity and purpose. "Our work joins us in knitting the garment of culture which we ourselves enjoy" (39). When people work together, and even when they engage in economic exchange, they join in common cause toward a shared goal. This implicitly recognizes the humanity of others. They recognize that they need each other.

Both sides of the ledger—work and wage—draw the executive stewardship of each individual into the service of the community. I take my job freely (rather than being forced to do a job that was chosen for me, as under socialist systems) and do the work as an expression of my own agency. I buy and sell as a steward of my money and goods, in a marketplace that is not under the arbitrary control of a central planner. Yet in both the work and the wage, the needs of my neighbors are served.

DeKoster asks us to consider how thousands of people, who don't even know each other, work together to create all the objects we use every day:

> That chair you are lounging in? Could you have made it for yourself? Well, I suppose so, *if* we mean just the chair! Perhaps you did in fact go out to buy the wood,

the nails, the glue, the stuffing, the springs—and put it all together. But if by making a chair we mean assembling each part *from scratch*, that's quite another matter. How do we get, say, the wood? Go and fell a tree? But only after first making the tools for that, and putting together some kind of vehicle to haul the wood, and constructing a mill to do the lumber, and roads to drive on from place to place? In short, a lifetime or two to make one chair! We are physically unable, it is obvious, to provide ourselves from scratch with the household goods we can now see from wherever you and I are sitting—to say nothing of building and furnishing the whole house.

Consider everything else that we can use every day and never really see. Who builds and maintains the roads and streets we take for granted? Who polices them so we can move about in comparative safety? Who erects the stores, landscapes the parks, builds the freeways? Who provides the services that keep things going in good weather and bad?

Well, civilization blends work together into all that.… There are countless workers, just like ourselves—including ourselves—whose work creates the harvest that provides each of us with far more than we could ever provide for ourselves. (3–4)

But here we must be very careful. Markets are not some machine that delivers good outcomes automatically. DeKoster was no pedantic peddler of economic ideology, treating systems as if they had no relationship to the people operating within them.

The whole package—shared work creating peace and harmony, markets reconciling freedom and community—works *only* if people possess moral character and the economic system is just. A nation of cheats and scoundrels is not going to grow more harmonious through shared work. And even the peace created by good people working together will be undermined if the system within which they work rewards cheats and scoundrels. We don't have to be perfect people or have a perfect system, but we do have to be good enough people with a good enough system.

Freedom, responsibility, and community are interdependent. The freedom to take what you want rather than serve the common good is not true freedom at all. As DeKoster pointedly asks:

> When are we "free" to use the highways? When we [all] drive as we please? No, *only* when most drivers maintain order by obeying most of the laws most of the time. Destroy the system so we drive as we please, and, of course, no one would really be free to use the road. (45)

True freedom is *voluntary lawfulness*. When people freely choose to work for one another's benefit, they are free to live in community. It is their responsibility to each other that sets them free.

With this perspective on freedom, we can recover our agency and responsibility even in situations where they seem the most lost. If freedom means the power to do whatever you want, factory workers have little of it. But if freedom is a voluntary lawfulness that chooses to serve the needs of others, they can find freedom in their work, and in the economic exchange their work empowers them for.

DeKoster's Three Dimensions of Work

While it seems simple and plainspoken on the surface, DeKoster's book actually invites us to view work as a complex, three-dimensional reality. These dimensions are neither simple nor straightforward in practice—real life always defies the simplicity of our schemes of classification. However, this three-dimensional rubric can help us intentionally broaden our thinking, and become aware of aspects of work that we may not have otherwise considered.

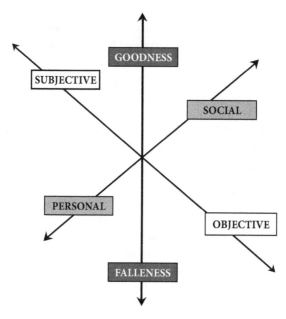

One dimension of our work is defined by the distinction between *objective* and *subjective*. No matter how pious your feelings about it are, it still matters to God whether your work is actually having a beneficial effect on other people. At the same time, human dignity and the shaping of the self for God can only be lived out if we do our work with the right sense of identity and motives. We see this dimension most clearly in DeKoster's twofold understanding of God's presence in our work—that we love God in our work by serving our neighbor (objectively) and shaping ourselves (subjectively).

The second dimension is defined by *goodness* and *fallenness*. Theologically, the goodness of God in our work must be primary, lest we compromise our conception of his transcendence or deny the gospel truth that Christ has overcome the world. But for many people, the daily experience of work is overwhelmed by the brokenness of the fall and the curse. The Christian virtue of hope addresses itself to the experience of suffering and evil with a message of victory and light.

The third dimension is defined by the *personal* and *social*. Each individual is an executive steward, with agency and responsibility. We must not turn inward and use our work or our wages as opportunities to serve ourselves, but must use them instead to serve the needs of our households and communities. The community, in turn, must honor each individual as an executive steward, sustaining systems of work and exchange that are just and provide the necessary context of freedom and responsibility.

The faith and work movement is reaching a new level of maturity. It first emerged among workers who felt called to affirm the goodness of God in their work. Now it is beginning to reach a wider world of workers—many of whom feel little connection to these cheerful affirmations. The hopeful, three-dimensional vision of Lester DeKoster can help the movement discover new directions for growth, shining the light of Christ into a dark and dying world.

Reflection Questions

1. DeKoster writes that he once thought the Parable of the Sheep and the Goats primarily referred to "special acts of giving, such as charities that we ought to be doing in our spare time." Why did he come to view this interpretation as inadequate?

2. How can the Parable of the Talents help us understand the Bible's strict work ethic as something beautiful that gives dignity and meaning to life, rather than as a mere pharisaical demand?

3. When speaking to people whose work is characterized by suffering or discouragement, what are some good starting points for connecting our message to their experience? What are appropriate goals for pastoral care of such workers?

4. Why does the ordinary worker need to be regularly reminded of how his work affects his community? Why do communities need to be regularly reminded of what their workers contribute?

About the Authors

Lester DeKoster (1915–2009) became director of the library at Calvin College and Seminary, affiliated with the Christian Reformed Church in North America, in 1951. He earned his doctorate from the University of Michigan in 1964, after completing a dissertation on "Living Themes in the Thought of John Calvin: A Bibliographical Study." During his tenure at the college, DeKoster was influential in expanding the holdings of what would become the H. Henry Meeter Center for Calvin Studies, one of the preeminent collections of Calvinist and Reformed texts in the world. DeKoster also amassed an impressive personal library of some ten thousand books, which includes a wide array of sources testifying to both the breadth and depth of his intellectual vigor. DeKoster was a professor of speech at the college and enjoyed taking up the part of historic Christianity and confessional Reformed theology in debates on doctrinal and social issues that pressed the church throughout the following decades. Both his public debates and private correspondence were marked by a spirit of charity that tempered and directed the needed words of rebuke. After his retirement from Calvin College in 1969, DeKoster labored for a decade as the editor of *The Banner*, the denominational magazine of the Christian Reformed Church. This position provided him with another platform from which to critically engage the life of the church and the world. During this time DeKoster also launched, in collaboration with Gerard Berghoef (a longtime elder in the church) and their families, the Christian's Library Press, a publishing endeavor intended to provide timely resources both for the church's laity and its leadership.

GREG FORSTER (PhD, Yale University) is a program director in the Faith, Work, and Economics Program at the Kern Family Foundation, a senior fellow at the Friedman Foundation for Educational Choice, and the editor of the group blog Hang Together. He is the author of several books, including *Joy for the World* (Crossway, 2014), *The Joy of Calvinism* (Crossway, 2014), *The Contested Public Square* (InterVarsity, 2008), and *John Locke's Politics of Moral Consensus* (Cambridge University Press, 2005). He contributes regularly to The Gospel Coalition, First Thoughts, and other online outlets.

STEPHEN J. GRABILL serves as Senior Research Scholar in Theology at the Acton Institute, a Grand Rapids, Michigan-based think tank that integrates Christian worldview with economics for leaders in the church, academy, and business sectors. He is editor emeritus of the *Journal of Markets & Morality*, as well as General Editor of the *NIV Stewardship Study Bible*, an Evangelical Christian Publishers Association (ECPA) award-contending resource, and a founding board member of Stewardship Council, the producer of the study Bible and a leader in the development and delivery of stewardship resources. Dr. Grabill graduated from Calvin Theological Seminary with a doctorate in systematic theology, after having spent more than a decade exploring the insights of the Reformed tradition on ethics, politics, and culture. He is author of *Rediscovering the Natural Law in Reformed Theological Ethics* (Eerdmans, 2006) and editor of *Sourcebook in Late-Scholastic Monetary Theory* (Lexington, 2007).

Christian's **LIBRARY PRESS**

Founded in 1979 by Gerard Berghoef and Lester DeKoster, **CHRISTIAN'S LIBRARY PRESS** has been committed to publishing influential texts on church leadership, the vocation of work, and stewardship for more than thirty years. During that time Berghoef and DeKoster wrote significant works including *The Deacons Handbook*, *The Elders Handbook*, and *God's Yardstick*, which still are in demand today. After the passing of Lester DeKoster in 2009, the imprint is now administered by the Acton Institute for the Study of Religion & Liberty. For more information about Christian's Library Press, visit www.clpress.com.

ACTON INSTITUTE

With its commitment to pursue a society that is free and virtuous, the **ACTON INSTITUTE FOR THE STUDY OF RELIGION & LIBERTY** is a leading voice in the international environmental and social policy debate. With offices in Grand Rapids, Michigan, and Rome, Italy, as well as affiliates in four other nations around the world, the Acton Institute is uniquely positioned to comment on the sound economic and moral foundations necessary to sustain humane environmental and social policies. The Acton Institute is a nonprofit, ecumenical think tank working internationally to "promote a free and virtuous society characterized by individual liberty and sustained by religious principles." For more on the Acton Institute, please visit www.acton.org.

CPSIA information can be obtained
at www.ICGtesting.com
Printed in the USA
FSHW011807090819